SAP SRM / Advanced EBP Cookbook

By Jim Stewart

For Farrah

ABOUT THE AUTHOR

Jim Stewart (Los Angeles, CA) has over 10 years of experience as an SAP consultant, during which time he has served as a functional lead, lead developer, and ABAP programmer. He has implemented SAP for The US Army, DirecTV, Texas Instruments, Hewlett Packard, and other Fortune 100 clients. Mr. Stewart is the founder of Equity Technology Group, an SAP consulting partner, and continues to practice as a consultant in the area of SAP SRM, Workflow, Web programming, and UNIX systems administration. Equity Technology Group is a leading provider of SRM implementation support and services.

Equity Technology Group

Tel: 951-788-0810

Fax: 951-788-0812

Email: fjstewart@equitytechgroup.com

www.equitytechgroup.com

Forward

What this book *isn't*:

This book isn't by any means complete or exhaustive. There will be a 2nd edition, and another book on SUS, Live Auction & Bidding, and probably a book covering Catalog issues.

What this book *is*:

This book will provide the reader with implementation techniques that are commonly reserved by consultants as "company internal," or as "secret." I'm not sure who came up with the term "secret handshake" but I've been using that term for a couple of years to describe key bits of knowledge that you *just have to know* to use a piece of software effectively. Somehow this information is never provided in the documentation, or if it is, it's hidden in the footnote of page 253 of a thousand-page, obscurely named reference. If you're working on SAP's SRM or EBP, this is certainly the right book for you. If you're already working in SRM, you know what I mean. It's also worth mentioning that in this book, you'll find introductory material that will serve as a good reference later, and you'll definitely find advanced material that will challenge you and your project teammates when you try for more involved solutions. I still use a dog-eared copy of these materials every day on my projects and give copies to all of my teammates (well, at least the one's I like).

There have been rumors that a cookbook existed for SAP SRM 4.0, which have been denied by SAP. I spoke with the product manager in September of 2004, and as far as he told me, there is no official SAP SRM cookbook. I think there have been cookbooks for earlier versions, none of which I can find on SAP's service website. But I have heard rumors that they do exist. In any case, regardless of any other books or documents, I'm hoping that this book will be the definitive cookbook for SRM and that I can write a more complete and updated versions as new functionality is released. And as more stable versions of SRM emerge and become widely used, this book might be broken into several parts based on version. But for now, this book is limited to mostly SRM version 3.0 and beyond, and as such should apply mostly to EBP versions 3.0, 3.5, 4.0, and 5.0. And it's all thrown in together.

Another important note about content and where the content for this book has come from.

This book represents notes, fixes, and documentation that I and other consultants have made and recorded on various high-profile SRM implementation projects, and notes that I've bartered from other consultants on different projects. I've traded for drinks, dinners or other hard to get pieces of information. I know that every single bit of information contained in this book has been used to help a customer meet its requirements. My only hope is that you'll find it as valuable as I and my clients have.

Jim Stewart

Boston, Massachusetts

Section 1: Configuration Guide

The configuration guide will be broken into two parts: SRM configuration and R3 configuration. The first section, SRM Configuration describes configuration that needs to be done on the SRM server side, so you can log in via the web and create shopping carts. Some of this configuration depends upon R3 configuration being there already – so make sure that the R3 backend system is in place and is completely configured. Data replication into SRM, in particular, depends upon the R3 configuration being complete. This configuration guide represents the SRM system working in a very simple scenario -- Classic mode. That is, shopping carts will be created and approved on the SRM system, and purchase orders or purchase requisitions (so called follow-on documents) are created on the backend R3 system.

SRM Configuration

The following configuration needs to be completed on the SRM server. The configuration is done on an SRM 4.0 (EBP 5.0) system and follows the order described here. Some of these steps may be taken out of order, and some steps require the backend configuration exists. In particular, the replication of master data from the backend relies on configuration and interoperability with the R3 backend.

Basis Steps

The following steps are typically completed by a part of the basis team – you can do them yourself, if you have the proper authorization.

1. Maintain Logical System for both the EBP client and R/3 client that EBP will be connected to in the EBP golden client as well as in the R/3 golden client. Use transaction SM59.
2. Create System users for running standard EBP reports and for Workflow Processing. Use transaction SU01.
3. Maintain RFC Destination for both the EBP client and R/3 client that EBP will be connected to in the EBP connected as well as in the R/3 connected client.
4. Activate the Standard Workflow Customizing using transaction SWU3 (especially the synchronization of the WF-BATCH user ID and password)
5. Set exit URL for the ITS to the SRM login page
6. Schedule standard system reports
7. Enable English language on ITS login page

Number Ranges

Number ranges must be established for EBP shopping carts as well as any potential purchasing document that can be generated in the backend R/3 system from EBP. For example, when a shopping cart is submitted to R/3, a requisition, reservation, purchase order or service order will be generated. The EBP system needs a number range established that automatically takes the next available number and assigns it to the document which will be created in R/3. Configuration must also be established in the R/3 system to correlate with the ranges setup in EBP so that a conflict never arises when a purchasing document is created directly in the R/3 system on a similar number range. This configuration is covered in a separate document.

Define Number Ranges for Shopping Carts

Transaction: SPRO

IMG: Supplier Relationship Management → SRM Server → Cross-Application Basic Settings → Number Ranges → SRM Server Number Ranges → Define Number Ranges for Shopping Carts and Follow-on Documents

Choose 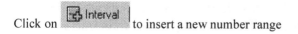 to change existing intervals for EBP shopping carts.

Click on ![Interval] to insert a new number range

	No	From number	To number	Current number	Ext	
	01	0010000000	0019999999	0	☐	

Ranges

Insert the Shopping Cart number range information from the chart above.

Save the number range.

Define Number Range for Goods Receipts

Transaction: SPRO

IMG: Supplier Relationship Management → SRM Server → Cross-Application Basic Settings → Number Ranges → SRM Server Number Ranges → Define Number Range for Local Confirmations of Services and Goods Receipts

Choose ⬛ Intervals to change existing intervals for EBP goods receipt tracking.

Click on ⬛ Interval to insert a new number range

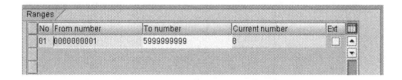

Insert the Local Goods Receipt number range information from the chart above.

Save the number range.

JIM STEWART

Vendor (Business Partner Number Ranges)

Transaction: BUCF

IMG: Cross Application components → SAP Business Partner → Business Partner → Basic settings → Number Ranges and Groupings → Define Number Ranges

Backend number range was set in numerical format. Adjusted the default character number range in EBP to a numeric number range in order to replicate vendor master records.

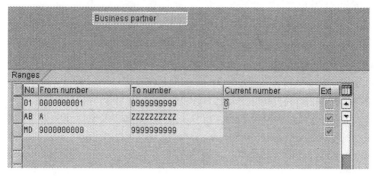

Initial settings for number ranges

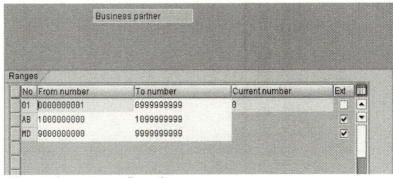

After number range configuration

Vendor List

Transaction: BBP_NUM_AVL

IMG: Supplier Relationship Management → SRM Server → Cross-Application Basic Settings → Number Ranges → Define Number Ranges for Vendor List.

Vendor lists in EBP are completely separate from traditional source lists in the R/3 backend system and must be setup on their own internal number range in the EBP system.

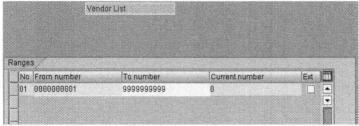

Definition of vendor list number range

Section E: Link Backend Number Ranges to EBP Ranges for Purchasing Documents

Transaction: SPRO

IMG: Supplier Relationship Management → SRM Server → Cross-Application Basic Settings → Number Ranges → SRM Server Number Ranges → Define Number Ranges per Backend system for Follow-on Documents

Entries should be created in the EBP system to link the EBP purchase orders, requisitions and reservations to the backend R/3 system. PO, RQ and RS were used to easily distinguish each number range defined in the next section. The logical system ID should reflect that of the EBP application server and client in which the number ranges are being configured.

Definition of No. Range Intervals for Documents in Backend			
LogSystem	Number Range POs	No. Range PReqs	No. Range Reservations
	PO	RQ	RS

Define Number Range for Backend Follow-on Documents

Transaction: SPRO

IMG: Supplier Relationship Management → SRM Server → Cross-Application Basic Settings → Number Ranges → SRM Server Number Ranges → Define Number Ranges for Shopping Carts and Follow-on Documents

Maintain internal number ranges for the purchase order (PO), purchase requisition (RQ), reservation (RS) and the service entry sheet (SE). These number ranges should exactly correlate with an external number range in the R/3 system for each types of purchasing document.

No	From number	To number	Current number	Ext
PO	4100000000	4199999999	0	☐
RQ	0090000000	0099999999	0	☐
RS	0030000000	0039999999	0	☐
SE	0200000000	0209999999	0	☐

Define Number Range for Local Bid Invitations

Transaction: SPRO

IMG: Supplier Relationship Management → SRM Server → Cross-Application Basic Settings → Number Ranges → SRM Server Number Ranges → Define Number Range for Local Bid Invitations

An internal number range must be defined to numerically build local bid invitations for RFQ's and Auctions in the Bidding Engine and Live Auction applications. These bids do not have a link to any R/3 purchasing documents; they are completely local to the EBP system.

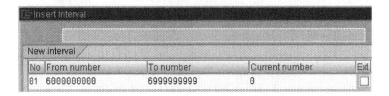

Define Number Range for Local Bids

Transaction: SPRO

IMG: Supplier Relationship Management → SRM Server → Cross-Application Basic Settings → Number Ranges → SRM Server Number Ranges → Define Number Range for Local Bids

Maintain an internal number range for local EBP bids received back from suppliers. This number range also contains no link to any R/3 purchasing documents.

No	From number	To number	Current number	Ext
01	8000000000	8999999999	0	☐

Define ITS URL

Transaction: SM30
Table: TWPURLSVR

Before the Internet Transaction Server can process EBP requests, entries in table TWPURLSVR must be maintained to initiate a connection to a physical URL. This URL controls the menu on the left hand side of the screen that houses all of the transactions users have access to.

The URL will vary depending on which EBP client the configuration is performed in. The URL should consist of base address for the Integrated ITS instance. This configuration should only need to be performed once for each client in which EBP purchasing will be enabled.

Choose **New Entries** to change existing intervals for EBP shopping carts.

Logical system	
Logical Web Servers for Logical Systems	
Web server	
Web protocol	HTTP
SAP GUI for HTML ID	
GUI start server	
GUI start protocol	HTTP

Fill in the ITS host and port numbers for the first 2 server entries and tag the protocols as 'http':

Maintain ITS URL

Middleware Setup for data transfer from R/3

Middleware is used on the SRM application to transfer and synchronize master data with an R/3 or multiple R/3 backend systems. In our case, only a single backend system will be used for replication with SRM, that being our R3 backend system. Example master data includes plants, commodity codes, material master records, etc.

This initial setup of middleware described in this document should only need to be processed in a new SRM client or re-validated when a client copy, system refresh or the existing backend system client is swapped out with a new or other client.

Define Product Master Output Length

Transaction: SPRO
IMG: Supplier Relationship Management → SRM Server →
Master Data → Products → Define Output Format and Storage
Form of Product Ids

The following configuration is necessary to replicate material master records into the EBP environment from R/3. The recommended output length by SAP is 18 characters.

1. Choose 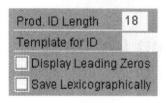 to create a product ID output length

2. Fill in the Product ID Length with 18 and save record

Prod. ID Length	18
Template for ID	
☐ Display Leading Zeros	
☐ Save Lexicographically	

Define Replication Site for Backend System

Transaction: SMOEAC

Transport: Not Transportable

Define a site within EBP that represents the backend system.

Choose Object Type  .

Click on ⬜ button to create a New site.

1. Specify a name and a description and choose R/3 from the Type drop-down list.

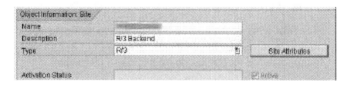

Click on the **Site Attributes** button to begin specifying the RFC Destination.

Choose the logical system name for the backend R/3 system in which data will be replicated/synchronized. Click on the green check mark to save the logical system.

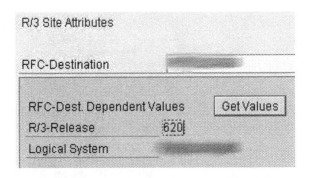

Click on the button to save the site definition.

End Result:

Define Replication Site for EBP System

Transaction: SMOEAC

Transport: Not Transportable

Update the site within EBP that represents the EBP system (CRM Entry).

Double click on the CRM Site Definition delivered with the system

Update the Site name and description to reflect the SRM Logical system ID and an EBP related description.

Click on the **Site Attributes** button to begin specifying the RFC Destination for the local EBP system.

Choose the logical system name for the EBP system. Click on the green check mark to save the logical system.

Click on the 🖫 button to save the site definition.

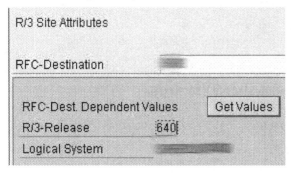

End Result:

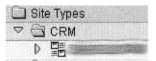

Maintain Middleware Parameters

Transaction: SM30

Table: SMOFPARSFA

This configuration is transportable.

Table SMOFPARSFA contains several parameters that exist to
drive how the middleware application should operate when
triggered either manually or automatically. Only one parameter
value must be created and maintained in the EBP system.

The following entry should be created in the EBP system in order to
link the EBP middleware to the backend EBP consumer object
created above.

Key	MCRM
Parameter Name	MCRM_CONSUMER
Param. Name 2	
Param. Name 3	

Middleware Parameter	
User	EBP
Param. Value	X
Param. Value 2	
Comment	
Created by	
Modification Date	
Changed by	
Date of Creation	

Save the Entry

Deactivate CRM Specific Settings

Transaction: SE38

Report: BBP_PRODUCT_SETTINGS_MW

This configuration is transportable.

Run report BBP_PRODUCT_SETTINGS_MW with the following criteria to deactivate CRM specific settings. Since the CRM and EBP applications once shared the same SAP core, this report is necessary to make sure only EBP relevant data is replicated over from R/3.

Consumer (EBP Only w/o CRM)   EBP

⦿ Service Product Active
◯ Service Product Inactive

☐ Test Mode

After the report is completed, you should get a successful output page similar to the following:

JIM STEWART

```
Middleware Settings for Product for EBP-Only Systems

Settings Log:                          EBP Without CRM

Set Middleware Objects to Active/Inactive
All Business Objects Except MATERIAL and DNL_PLANT Will Be Set to Inactive
All Customizing Objects Except DNL_CUST_PROD0/_PROD1 Will Be Set to Inacti
All Condition Objects Will Be Set to Inactive
Objects SERVICE_MASTER and DNL_CUST_SRVMAS Will Also Be Activated

User of Download Objects Will Be Adjusted (Table SMOFINICON)

Object:     MATERIAL
Following Tables Will Be Deactivated:
  MLAN
  MVKE
  STXH
  STXL

Object:     DNL_CUST_PROD1
Following Tables Will Be Deactivated:
  T179
  T179T

Middleware Objects Will Be Regenerated

Adjustments in the Central Middleware Settings (Table SMOFSUBTAB)
  CRMGENERAL LOG_LEVEL            *                         —> T
  FLOW       FLOWTRACE_ACTIVE                               —> X
  DEVSYSTEM  DEVSYSTEM                                      —> X
  R3A_COMMON CRM_VERSION_ACTIVE     SYNCHRONOUS_CALL   1.2  —> X X

EBP Will Be Flagged As Active Application (Table SMOFAPPL)
CRM Will Be Flagged As Inactive Application (Table SMOFAPPL)


Customizing Indicator 'Multiple-Backends' Set (Table COMC_HIERARCHY)
```

Set Filter to Exclude Material Groups

Transaction: R3AC3

Customizing Object: DNL_CUST_PROD1

Transport: Not Transportable

Filters can set to include or exclude specific product categories (material groups) from being replicated over to the EBP system from the R/3 system. We will replicate only the UNSPSC codes selected for this example configuration. All others will be excluded. These entries are not transportable because they are directly tied to the R/3 client specified by the Site Name chosen for the filter. When the filter is generated in the EBP system, the filter settings are transferred to a table in the R/3 client so when new categories are created or existing ones are changed, the R/3 system knows which records to consider for replication.

Tip: The filter values in table t023 and t023t must match exactly for the filters to operate properly when customizing object DNL_CUST_PROD1 is initiated.

Select on the DNL_CUST_PROD1 line and click on the ![icon] to choose the customizing entry.

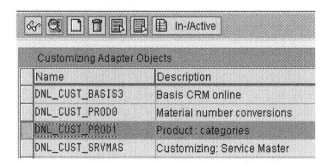

Click on the ![pencil] button to switch to change mode.

Click on the ![Tables/Structures] tab to go to the Product Category Table definitions.

Click on the **Filter Settings** button for the line with table T023
specified as the Source Site.

Choose the Site name that was created in Section B for the backend
R/3 client.

Source Site Name	<CHOOSE A SITE NAME>
	<CHOOSE A SITE NAME>

Make sure the option 'Filter in source and target database' is
selected in the Filter Option field.

Source Site Name	
Filter Option	Filter in source and target database

Specify all of the product categories line by line which should be
excluded from the product category replication to keep the EBP
system clean. In this example, all PLM-SCM categories were
excluded.

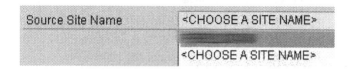

Table/structure name	T023			Regenerate Filter	
Filter Settings					
Field	OP	LOW	HIGH	Incl/Excl	
MATKL	Inequality (<> Low)	10010		Inclusive defined set/a	
MATKL	Inequality (<> Low)	10020		Inclusive defined set/a	
MATKL	Inequality (<> Low)	10030		Inclusive defined set/a	
MATKL	Inequality (<> Low)	10040		Inclusive defined set/a	
MATKL	Inequality (<> Low)	10050		Inclusive defined set/a	
MATKL	Inequality (<> Low)	10060		Inclusive defined set/a	
MATKL	Inequality (<> Low)	10070		Inclusive defined set/a	
MATKL	Inequality (<> Low)	10080		Inclusive defined set/a	

Repeat the steps for table T023T with the same settings and values.

Table/structure name	T023T				Regenerate Filter
Filter Settings					
Field	OP		LOW	HIGH	Incl/Excl
MATKL	Inequality (<> Low)		10010		Inclusive defined set/ai
MATKL	Inequality (<> Low)		10020		Inclusive defined set/ai
MATKL	Inequality (<> Low)		10030		Inclusive defined set/ai
MATKL	Inequality (<> Low)		10040		Inclusive defined set/ai
MATKL	Inequality (<> Low)		10050		Inclusive defined set/ai
MATKL	Inequality (<> Low)		10060		Inclusive defined set/ai
MATKL	Inequality (<> Low)		10070		Inclusive defined set/ai
MATKL	Inequality (<> Low)		10080		Inclusive defined set/ai

Definition of backend systems connected to the EBP client

A backend definition must be defined for the Live Auction application since it is not housed directly on the same EBP application server as well at the R/3 client that the EBP system will be connected to in a Classic mode.

Define Link to Live Auction System

Transaction: SPRO

IMG Location: Supplier Relationship Management → SRM Server → Technical Basic Settings → Define Backend Systems

Transport Not Transportable

In the logical system field, specify the logical system created for the Live Auction application by the Basis team.

Logical sys
LIVAUCTION

Choose a description for the system in which EBP will communicate with and specify the RFC Destination that was established by the Basis team (SM59).

Description	RFC Destination
Live Auction	SRM_LIVE_AUCTION

Choose "SRM Live Auction" for the System Type.

Sys. type
SRM Live Auction

Save the entry.

Logical system	Description	RFC Destination	Sys. type
LIVAUCTION	Live Auction	SRM_LIVE_AUCTION	SRM Live Auction

Define Link to R/3 Enterprise System

Transaction: SPRO

IMG Location: Supplier Relationship Management → SRM Server → Technical Basic Settings → Define Backend Systems

Maintain the Backend Logical System ID in the first field, insert a description to describe the R/3 system and link the RFC Destination (SM59 entry) that was created to connect to the R/3 system.

Logical system	Description	RFC Destination
	R/3 Backend	

Choose the 4.7 R/3 system in the System Type field, click on the RFC check box to indicate the system is RFC compatible and choose the real-time validation option in the FI Valid field.

Sys. type	R	Local	FI valid
R/3 system - version 4.70 ☑	☑	☐	real-time backend validation

Leave the remaining fields blank and save the record.

Create a Definition for Local EBP Document Processing

Transaction: SPRO

IMG Location: Supplier Relationship Management → SRM Server → Technical Basic Settings → Define Backend Systems

Maintain the Local Logical System ID in the first field, insert a description to describe the EBP system and link the RFC Destination (SM59 entry) that was created to connect to the EBP system.

Logical system	Description	RFC Destination
	Local	

Choose the Local B2B system in the System Type field, click on the Local check box to indicate the system is locally compatible and choose the real-time validation option in the FI Valid field.

Sys. type	R	Local	FI valid
Local B2B system ☑	☐	☑	real-time backend validation

Leave the remaining fields blank and save the record.

Create Root Org Structure Nodes

A root organizational unit must be created as a basis for the entire operational org structure for user default settings, workflow approvals, etc. The root organizational unit should only need to be created one time for each EBP client where shopping cart activity is performed unless the organizational structure is transported to production via ALE. A separate root org unit is recommended by SAP to house the vendor master records. Section A covers the creation of the purchasing root org unit and the Section B the supplier root org unit.

Create Root Organizational Unit for Purchasing Needs

Transaction: PPOCA_BBP

Transport: **Not transportable through SAP transports, but possible via ALE**

This step is to be performed one time in each EBP client where shopping will be enabled. Once the Root organizational unit is created, it can be accessed and further built upon from transaction PPOMA_BBP.

Leave the default dates of today and 12/31/9999 for the activate date range to be applied to the organizational unit.

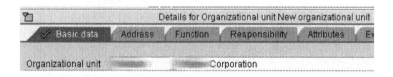

Click on the ✔ button to continue.

Maintain a short and long text for the organizational unit.

🗂	Details for Organizational unit New organizational unit

| ✔ Basic data | Address | Function | Responsibility | Attributes | Ex |

Organizational unit ▬▬▬ ▬▬Corporation

Click on the **Address** tab.

Maintain the an address for the organizational unit. Each org unit should always have an address maintained. In this example the corporate address was maintained. This address will most likely never be used, as users will probably be attached to lower levels of the org structure. Regardless, in the rare event that this address may be adopted as a delivery address, a realistic address should be specified.

Click on the 💾 button to save the org unit. Once generated, the org unit can be further maintained in transaction PPOMA_BBP.

Create Root Org Unit for Supplier Master Records

Transaction: PPOCA_BBP

Transport Not transportable through SAP transports, but possible via ALE

This step is to be performed one time in each EBP client where vendor master records will be replicated from an R/3 system to EBP. Once the Root organizational unit is created, it can be accessed from transaction PPOMA_BBP where additioanal org units can be arranged to house the various vendor master records.

Leave the default dates of today and 12/31/9999 for the activate date range to be applied to the organizational unit.

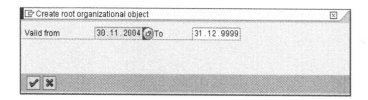

Click on the ✔ button to continue.

Maintain a short and long text for the organizational unit.

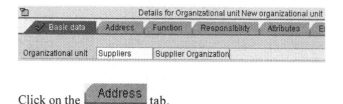

Click on the **Address** tab.

Maintain the an address for the organizational unit. Each org unit should always have an address maintained. In this example the corporate address was maintained. This address should never be used in transaction processing.

Click on the button to save the org unit. Once generated, the org unit can be further maintained in transaction PPOMA_BBP.

Transfer of non-material master R/3 master data

Transfer of non-material master from the R/3 system to the EBP system including data such as product categories, currency conversion rates, units of measure, etc.

Middleware is used on the SRM application to transfer and synchronize master data with an R/3 or multiple R/3 backend systems. In our case, only a single backend system will be used for replication with SRM, that being the R3 backend system. Example master data includes plants, commodity codes, material master records, etc.

Data replication should be performed after each client refresh, system copy or for new clients. A replication of data will override any manual settings performed in the EBP system since the initial replication. For example, if a currency rate was manually adjusted in the EBP system, when a delta or new initial replication is run, this adjusted value will be overwritten with the R/3 value.

Initial Download of Customizing Objects

Transaction: R3AS
Objects: DNL_CUST_BASIS3, DNL_CUST_PROD0,
DNL_CUST_PROD1, DNL_CUST_SRVMAS

Customizing Object Overview
DNL_CUST_BASIS3: Replicates currency conversion rates from the R/3 system.
DNL_CUST_PROD0: Material Master customizing object (sets product lengths to be replicated, not the physical material masters themselves)
DNL_CUST_PROD1: Replicates new product categories and updates to existing categories
DNL_CUST_SRVMAS: Service master customizing object.

Maintain the customizing objects outlined above in the Load Object field as single values and click on the green check mark to continue.

Click on the ⊕ to adopt the entries.

Enter in the backend logical system ID in the Source Site field and the EBP logical system ID in the Destination Site field that were defined in transaction SMOEAC.

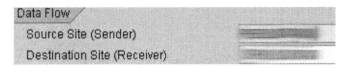

Click on the ⊕ to start the download.

A pop-up box should appear showing that the download for the customizing objects has started.

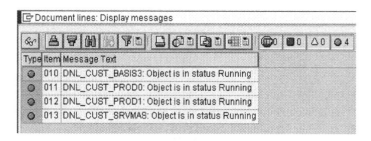

Monitor Download

Transaction: R3AM1

Execute transaction R3AM1.

Leave the search variables as defaulted and click on the 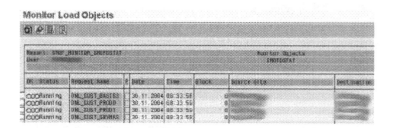 to get the status of the download.

If the Status of the customizing objects is yellow for more than a few minutes, something is either wrong with the middleware configuration or one of the download queues is stuck and needs to be manually pushed.

Middleware Troubleshooting – Stuck Queue in R/3

Transactions: SMQ1 (R/3)

Transport : Not Transportable

The first thing that should be checked when downloading customizing objects is a possible stuck queue. The EBP system primarily uses the Inbound queue (SMQ2) whereas the R/3 system uses the Outbound queue (SMQ1). The outbound queue is more often than not the queue that gets stuck initially.

First launch the Outbound Queue (SMQ1) in the R/3 System

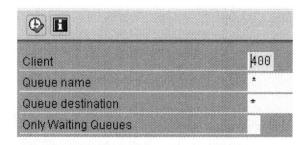

Click on the ⊕ button to view all queues.

If queues beginning with "R3A" are present, then they are probably stuck in a ready state and need to be manually kicked off.

SAP SRM ADVANCED EBP COOKBOOK

C1	Queue name	Destination	Entries
	R3AD_DNL_CUST_BASIS3*		1
	R3AD_DNL_CUST_PROD0*		1
	R3AD_DNL_CUST_PROD1*		1
	R3AD_DNL_CUST_SRVMAS*		1

Double click on the queue entry with "PROD0" in the name.

If the entry has "Stop" in the Status column, then place the cursor somewhere on the line and click on the 🔓 button to unlock the queue.

If the Destination field is not populated with the EBP logical system, than something is missing in the Middleware configuration and must be fixed. Otherwise, enter through this pop-up screen.

Unlock queue	
Queue name	R3AD_DNL_CUST_PROD0*
Destination	

Once the queue is unlocked, it can now be activated. Place the cursor on the line again and click on the ▮ button to activate the queue.

Again, enter through the pop-up.

The queue should disappear from the screen:

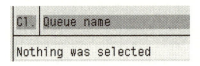

Repeat the above steps for the remaining customizing objects in the following order:

R3AD_DNL_CUST_PROD1, R3AD_DNL_CUST_BASIS3, R3AD_DNL_CUST_SRVMAS

Once all of the queues are completed, the will most likely need to be activated in the Inbound queue in the EBP system. Refer to the next section for the processing steps.

Middleware Troubleshooting – Stuck Queue in EBP

Transactions: SMQ2 (EBP)

Transport : Not Transportable

If the Outbound queue was stuck in Section C, then most likely the Inbound queues in EBP are waiting to be manually activated.

First launch the Outbound Queue (SMQ2) in the EBP System

qRFC Monitor (Inbound Queue)

Client	
QNAME	*
Waiting Queues Only	

Click on the ⊕ button to view all queues.

If queues beginning with "R3A" are present, then they are probably stuck in a ready state and need to be manually kicked off.

Number of Displayed Entries: 14
Number of Displayed Queues: 4

Cl.	Queue Name	Entries
400	R3AI_DNL_CUST_BASIS3	10
400	R3AI_DNL_CUST_PROD0	1
400	R3AI_DNL_CUST_PROD1	2
400	R3AI_DNL_CUST_SRVMAS	1

Double click on the queue entry with "PROD0" in the name.

If the entry has "Ready" in the Status column, then place the cursor somewhere on the line and click on the ▯ button to activate the queue.

Enter through the pop-up screen that appears.

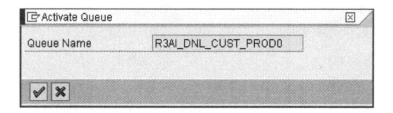

Click on the 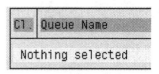 button until the queue is cleared from the screen.

If the following does not eventually appear on the screen, there is a larger problem with the replication. Check short dumps first for possible troubleshooting.

Cl.	Queue Name
Nothing selected	

Repeat the above steps for the remaining customizing objects in the following order:

R3AD_DNL_CUST_PROD1, R3AD_DNL_CUST_BASIS3, R3AD_DNL_CUST_SRVMAS

Replicate plants from R/3

Replicate plants from R/3 to EBP as business partners

Before a user can operate in the Classic mode, the plants must be replicated from the R/3 system to the EBP system. Not only does this speed up processing time, it provides better tracking through business partner relationships.

The steps outlined in section A will stop the following error from occurring when running the location replication report:

Ty	Message Text
■	Erroneous/Incomplete Data Record: Plant ▓▓▓ System ▓▓▓
■	Erroneous/Incomplete Data Record: Plant ▓▓▓ System ▓▓▓
■	The region ▓▓▓ s not defined for country ▓▓
■	Error Creating Location Plant ▓▓▓ System ▓▓▓
■	Erroneous/Incomplete Data Record: Plant ▓▓▓ System ▓▓▓

Prepare System Parameter for Location Replication

Transaction: SE38
Program: BBP_ATTR_XPRA400
This configuration is not transportable.

Run report BBP_ATTR_XPRA400

Ensure you receive a result list back similar to the following:

```
Conversion of the organizational attributes
Client 000: Start of conversion on 30.11.2004 at 09:57:30
Conversion already complete
Client 000: End of conversion on 30.11.2004 at 09:57:30
Client 066: Start of conversion on 30.11.2004 at 09:57:30
Conversion already complete
Client 066: End of conversion on 30.11.2004 at 09:57:30
Client 100: Start of conversion on 30.11.2004 at 09:57:30
Conversion already complete
Client 100: End of conversion on 30.11.2004 at 09:57:30
Client 200: Start of conversion on 30.11.2004 at 09:57:30
Conversion already complete
Client 200: End of conversion on 30.11.2004 at 09:57:30
Client 300: Start of conversion on 30.11.2004 at 09:57:30
Conversion already complete
Client 300: End of conversion on 30.11.2004 at 09:57:30
Client 400: Start of conversion on 30.11.2004 at 09:57:30
Conversion already complete
Client 400: End of conversion on 30.11.2004 at 09:57:30
Client 500: Start of conversion on 30.11.2004 at 09:57:30
Conversion already complete
Client 500: End of conversion on 30.11.2004 at 09:57:30
Conversion of the organizational attributes complete
```

Replicate Locations

Transaction: SE38

Program: BBP_LOCATIONS_GET_FROM_SYSTEM

Transport Not Transportable

Three different reports are available to replicate plants from the R/3 system. Aside from the one provided above which gets all locations from a specific system, you can use BBP_LOCATIONS_GET_ALL which will read all of the backend systems maintained in the IMG and gather all of the plants within these systems or BBP_LOCATIONS_GET_SELECTED to selectively choose which plants and which systems to replicate plants from.

Run the program and select the logical system ID of the R/3 system.

Click on the ⊕ button to execute the program.

You should receive a pop-up message to check SLG1 for any processing errors.

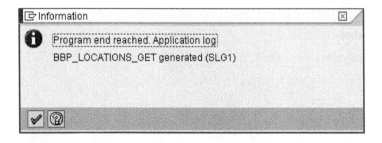

Check transaction SLG1 and take actions to correct any error messages you may receive. After fixing the cause of the error, run the replication program again to successfully transfer the plants that came over in error.

Run Program to Set Migration Indicator

Transaction: SE38

Program: BBP_LOCATION_MIGRATION_SET

Transport: Not Transportable

The follow error will occur in the organizational structure (ppoma_bbp) if the migration parameter is not set to X for denoting the plant locations have been successfully migrated from R/3. To alleviate this error the above program must be run to set the indicator. If the indicator must be reversed for some reason program BBP_LOCATION_MIGRATION_RESET can be run to set the value back to null.

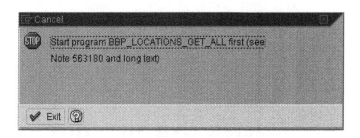

Enter in BBP_LOCATION_MIGRATION_SET in the program name field and hit F8 to execute the report.

Choose "Yes" on the following pop-up to proceed.

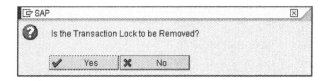

A successful message similar to the following should display. Return to PPOMA_BBP and verify that the location attributes can now be accessed.

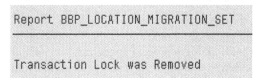

Build Skeleton Org Structure

Create Skeleton Structure for Users

Transaction: PPOMA_BBP

Transport Not transportable through SAP transports, but possible via ALE

A root organizational unit must be created prior to completing the configuration in this document. The skeleton structure must be developed in order to prepare for maintaining all attribute assignments and uploading users and buyers into the organizational environment.

This step is to be performed one time in each EBP client where shopping will be enabled. Once the Root organizational unit is created, it can be accessed and further built upon from transaction PPOMA_BBP.

Click on the root organizational unit created for purchasing purposes.

Click on the button to start creating a child org unit.

Select the link 'Is line supervisor of' in the pop-up box.

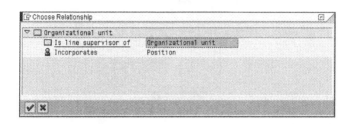

Define a short and long text to describe the org unit.

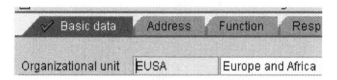

Maintain the address for the organizational unit. Each org unit should always have an address maintained. In this example the corporate address was maintained. This address will most likely never be used, as users will probably be attached to lower levels of the org structure. Regardless, in the rare event that this address may be adopted as a delivery address, a realistic address should be specified.

Click on the 💾 button to save the org unit.

Repeat the above steps to construct the remaining skeleton structure for purchasing hierarchy and once again for the purchasing organziation hierarchy.

Initial Settings for Integrating Business Partners

Once the skeleton organizational structure is in place, steps must be taken to create business partner relationships for each org unit. A user or supplier record cannot be assigned to an organizational unit until it has a business partner record generated.

Prior to establishing the Business parter relationships for organizational units, the column within the organizational structure will be blank.

When Business Partner relationships are not established, users cannot be imported into the organizational structure from the Users_Gen transaction. The following error results:

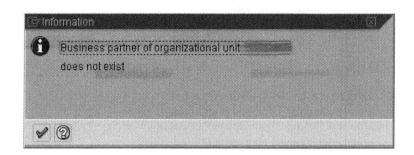

Define Parameters for Organizational Structure Management

Transaction: SPRO

IMG: Supplier Relationship Management → Cross-Application Basic Settings → Organizational Management → Integration Business Partner-Organizational Management → Set Up Integration with Organizational Management

These settings are transportable.

Ensure the following settings are established for local HR maintenance within the Enterprise Buyer system. These settings need only be established in the initial configuration of an SRM client. SAP recommended setting the X for the HRAC parameter to allow proper transfer of address changes in the organizational environment with the business partner records.

System Switch (from Table T77S0)			
Group	Sem. abbr.	Value abbr.	Description
HRALX	HRAC	X	Activate HR Integration
HRALX	OADBP		Business Partner of Standard Address
HRALX	OADRE		Address Necessary for Business Partner?
HRALX	OBPON	ON	Integration O-BP Activated
HRALX	OBWIG	X	Ignore Business Partner Warnings
HRALX	ONUMB	1	Business Partner Number Assignment (Org. Unit)
HRALX	OSUBG		Business Partner Subgroup (Organizational Unit)
HRALX	PBPHR	CREATE	Employees Are Replicated from HR System
HRALX	PBPON	ON	Integration Employee/BP Activated
HRALX	PCATS		Integration P-BP for CATS Activated
HRALX	PNUMB	1	Business Partner Number Assignment (Employee)
HRALX	PQUAL		Import Qualifications
PLOGI	PLOGI	01	Integration Plan Version / Active Plan Version
PLOGI	PRELI	99999999	Integration: default position

SAP SRM ADVANCED EBP COOKBOOK

Create Business Partner Relationships for Organizational Objects

Transaction: SPRO

IMG: Supplier Relationship Management → Cross-Application Basic Settings → Organizational Management → Integration Business Partner-Organizational Management → Match Up Organizational Units and Persons with Business Partners

Click on the Organizational Unit(s) field lookup 🔲 button to select a group of organizational units to establish business partners for or leave blank to gather all org units that need business partners generated. With the initial skeleton build of the org structure, leave the field blank and skip to step 5.

Click the checkbox next to the root org unit.

Name	ID	Code
▽ ☐ Organizational structure		
▽ ☐ ☑ ▢▢▢▢▢▢	O 5000▢	Global
▽ ☐ ☐ ▢▢▢ Placeholder for exp	O 500▢	▢▢▢▢▢
☐ ☐ United States	O 500▢	US
☐ ☐ Europe	O 5000▢	Europe
☐ ☐ Suppliers	O 5000▢	Suppliers
▷ ☐ ☐ Purchasing Departmen	O 500▢	Purchasing

Click on the 🔲 button to trigger a select all for the organizational units residing below the root org unit.

64

JIM STEWART

Name	ID	Code
▽ 🗀 Organizational structure		
▽ ☐ ☑ ▬▬ Global	O 5000▬	Global
▽ ☐ ☑ ▬ Placeholder for exp	O 50000▬	▬
☐ ☑ United States	O 5000▬	US
☐ ☑ Europe	O 5000▬	Europe
☐ ☑ Suppliers	O 5000▬	Suppliers
▷ ☐ ☑ Purchasing Departmen	O 50000▬	Purchasing

Click on the ☑ button to continue.

Click on the check box next to the Organizational Unit(s) field to select org units for sychronization processing.

☑ Organizational Unit(s)

Click on the ⊕ button to obtain the business partner status' of the selected org units.

Object Overview

Type	Number	Abbreviation	Partner Number	Basic Data	Address	Bank D
O	⬚ 5000▬			■	■	
O	50000▬	Suppliers		■	■	
O	50000▬	EU-AFRICA		■	■	
O	50000▬	Europe		■	■	
O	50000▬	UK		■		
O	50000▬	▬		■	■	
O	5000000▬	▬		■	■	
O	50000▬	PORGS		■	■	
O	50000▬	EU-AFRICA		■	■	
O	50000▬	Europe		■	■	
O	5000▬	▬		■	■	
O	5000▬	Electrical		■	■	
O	5000▬	Software		■	■	
O	5000▬	Service		■	■	

TIP: If you see any records where an Address is maintained, it is highly recommended that an address be maintained for the org unit before the BP generation process is started. Org unit 50000005 in the example above falls under this category.

Click on the 🖺 button on the right half of the screen to select all records.

Click on the 🔡 button to start the synchronization process for all objects shown in the above report.

If any errors occur, go to the organizational structure to fix the org unit(s) and rerun this report to estalish the business partner relationships for those in error.

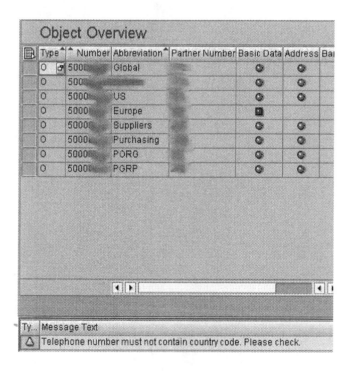

JIM STEWART

Assign attributes in the org structure

Assign all general attributes in the org structure that are inherited by all lower levels.

Organizational attributes serve many purposes in the EBP system. The primary purpose is to set attributes that define the users experience when shopping. Some example attributes are company codes, plants and cost centers that a user can order against.

This configuration document only covers the attributes that are mostly general in nature and where the same value is inherited by all users. The more general attributes that can be assigned at the highest level of the org structure is in direct correlation with the amount of organizational structure maintenance that is necessary in the initial configuration as well as future changes to the structure.

Maintain Accounting System Alias Attribute (ACS)

Transaction: PPOMA_BBP

Transport: Not transportable

This value is assigned to designate which system the accounting validation should be performed for any assignment to cost objects. The value should only need to be setup once at the highest organizational unit since all financial validations will occur in the backend R/3 system.

Double-Click on the root organizational unit created for purchasing purposes.

In the window that appears on the bottom of the screen, click on the Attributes tab.

Search for the 'System Alias for Accounting System' or 'ACS' attribute in the list.

	Description	Attribute	Exclu	Default	Inherit	Value
	System Alias for Accounting Systems	ACS	☐	☐	☐	

Maintain the logical system for the R/3 system in the Value field.

	Description	Attribute	Exclu	Default	Inherit	Value
	System Alias for Accounting Systems	ACS	☐	☐	☐	▬▬▬

Click on the 🖫 button to save the new attribute value.

Maintain Backend Document Type (BSA)

Transaction: PPOMA_BBP
Transport: Not transportable

The BSA (document type in R/3 system) organizational attribute links an EBP shopping cart to a document type in R/3 for purchase requisitions and purchase orders in R/3. A single document type 'ECPO' should be defined in the R/3 client which the EBP system is connected to by the MM team. This is the value that should be defined for the backend document type preceeded by the logical system and a backslash.

With this value set, any requisitions or purchase order generated in R/3 from EBP shopping carts will be tied to document type ECPO.

Repeat the steps 1-4 in Section A for the BSA attribute and attribute value.

Description	Attribute	Excl.	Default	Inhert	Value
Document Type in R/3 System	BSA	☐	☐	☐	ECPO

Click on the ⊞ button to save the new attribute value.

Maintain Company Code (BUK)

Transaction: PPOMA_BBP

Transport: Not transportable

A company code Local definition must be created at the highest level in the org structure where possible shop users may be placed for procurement processes. The BUK (company code) attribute can be set at the lower levels to direct users to more appropriate company code assignments.

In the steps below, a company code is set at the UK level as 1240. This configuration will probably need to be adjusted as part of any later migration with a more appropriate default value.

This Local attribute definition for company code is the key to defining allowable delivery addresses for a given location. In order for users to have the ability to look up addresses from a list, this attribute must be set and the "Edit Internal Addresses" transaction must be used to create the list.

Double-Click on the highest organizational unit that represents a legal entity.

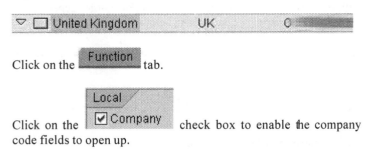

Click on the **Function** tab.

Click on the **☑ Company** check box to enable the company code fields to open up.

In the field on the far right with the drop-down list, choose the backend logical system in which the company code is defined.

In the company code field, enter the value of the company code that relates to the org unit being maintained.

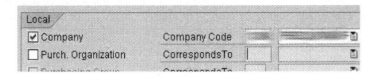

Click on the 🖫 button to save the company code definition.

Maintain Movement Type Attribute (BWA)

Transaction: PPOMA_BBP

Transport Not transportable

The movement type organizational attribute is set with value 201 to handle reservations. Even though reservations are not in scope for the Our implementation, it is necessary to maintain the attribute if the default material group for a given user or site is set to a backend logical system. The EBP system knows that if the user is set for backend procurement, that there might be a possibility for a reservation to be generated, therefore it checks to see that a value for this attribute is maintained. The BWA value should be defined for the as 201 preceeded by the logical system and a backslash.

Repeat the steps 1-4 in Section A for the BWA attribute and attribute value.

	Description	Attribute	Endu	Default	Inherit	Value
	Movement type	BWA	☐	☐	☐	201

Click on the 💾 button to save the new attribute value.

Local Currency Attribute (CUR)

Transaction: PPOMA_BBP
Transport: Not transportable

The local currency controls what currency the requisitioners see their shopping cart pricing in. If a catalog item is pulled in that is not equal to their local currency attribute, the currency will be converted in the EBP system using the conversion rates replicated over from the R/3 system (which are actually published from the MONEX legacy application). The local currency is an important attribute in driving approval processes to trigger for the local spend and approval limits per region.

Double-Click on the organizational unit created for purchasing purposes for the country where a local currency will need to be defined.

Repeat the steps 24 in Section A for the BWA attribute and attribute value. A lookup feature is available on the Value field for this attribute to locate the appropriate currency code.

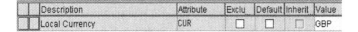

	Description	Attribute	Exclu	Default	Inherit	Value
	Local Currency	CUR	☐	☐	☐	GBP

Click on the Default check box to ensure that an inherited values are not taken over the lower level defaults.

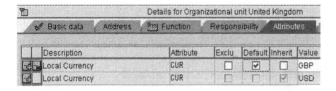

Details for Organizational unit United Kingdom

✔ Basic data	Address	Function	Responsibility	Attributes

	Description	Attribute	Exclu	Default	Inherit	Value
	Local Currency	CUR	☐	☑	☐	GBP
	Local Currency	CUR	☐	☐	☑	USD

Click on the ⊟ button to save the new attribute value.

Repeat the steps for each country and also set USD at the root organizational unit to serve as the global operating currency decided upon in your design.

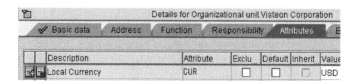

	Description	Attribute	Exclu	Default	Inherit	Value
	Local Currency	CUR	☐	☐	☐	USD

Maintain Forward Work Item Attribute (FORWARD_WI)

Transaction: PPOMA_BBP

Transport: Not transportable

The forward work item attribute when flagged, automatically sends approval notifications from the user's SAP inbox to their Outlook (or other external) mailbox. According to the Global key decisions defined, this attribute should be set to forward all work items. The exclusion checkbox can be used to stop the forwarding if necessary for a given user or group of users.

Repeat the steps 1-4 in Section A for the FORWARD_WI attribute and attribute value.

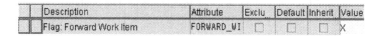

	Description	Attribute	Exclu	Default	Inherit	Value
	Flag: Forward Work Item	FORWARD_WI	☐	☐	☐	X

Click on the 🖫 button to save the new attribute value.

Maintain Current ITS of User (ITS_DEST)

Transaction: PPOMA_BBP

Transport: Not transportable

The ITS_DEST attribute is used to build the URL to go into the emails to approvers that they can click to launch the SRM application to review the approval item. This attribute will be set with the ITS for the EBP. This will need to be revisited with the Enterprise Portals application.

Repeat the steps 1-4 in Section A for the ITS_DEST attribute and attribute value.

Description	Attribute	Exclu	Default	Inherit	Value
Current ITS of User	ITS_DEST				

Click on the 💾 button to save the new attribute value.

Maintain Account Assignment Categories (KNT)

Transaction: PPOMA_BBP

Transport: Not transportable

The account assignment categories that a user is able to order against are maintained with the KNT attribute. At a minimum, cost center purchasing will be enabled for all users. The attribute therefore for our system will be setup at the root organizational level.

Repeat the steps 1-3 in Section A for the KNT attribute and attribute value.

In the KNT value field, either click on the search help button or hit F4 to look at the list of possible values.

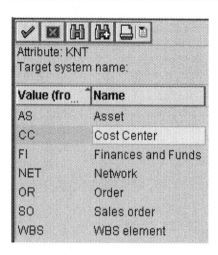

Double-click on the Cost Center account assignment entry to adopt this value.

	Description	Attribute	Exclu	Default	Inherit	Value
	Account assignment category	KNT	☐	☐	☐	CC

Click on the 🖫 button to save the new attribute value.

Maintain System Alias Attribute (SYS)

Transaction: PPOMA_BBP

Transport Not transportable

The SYS (system alias) organizational attribute controls the list displays in the central invoice and goods receipt transactions for a particular system. If a system value is not set for this attribute, the records for that system will not be displayed for the users within these transactions. For example, if an R/3 PO is created and the logical system for that Purchase Order is not configured with the

SYS attribute, the user will not see his/her PO in the goods receipt transaction and therefore cannot post a goods issue. The attribute is maintained at the root level in the organizational structure because all EBP users will be posting purchase order and goods receipts to a single backend R/3 system.

Repeat the steps 1-4 in Section A for the SYS attribute and attribute value.

Description	Attribute	Exclu	Default	Inherit	Value
System Alias	SYS	☐	☐	☐	

Click on the 🖫 button to save the new attribute value.

Maintain Systems for Vendor Master Records (VENDOR_ACS, VENDOR_SYS)

Transaction: PPOMA_BBP

Transport: Not transportable

Similar to the ACS accounting system reference attribute, the vendor_acs and vendor_sys attributes are used to determine which system to validate vendor accouting for and vendor master records. Since all vendor data will be resident in the R/3 backend system, both attributes should be set to the logical system of the backend system client in which the vendor master records will be or are replicated from.

Repeat the steps 1-4 in Section A for the SYS attribute and attribute value.

Description	Attribute	Exclu	Default	Inherit	Value
Accounting System for Vendor	VENDOR_ACS	☐	☐	☐	
System Alias for Vendor	VENDOR_SYS	☐	☐	☐	

Click on the button to save the new attribute value.

Define backend system for product categories

The product category drives which system requisitions, purchase orders, contracts, goods receipts, invoices, and contracts eventually flow into. This configuration is required for each product category before a user can order with the category.

There are two ways this configuration can be setup. Each category can be configured separately or a * can be used to denote that all categories follow the same path. Unless there are plans to stray from the Classic EBP mode to De-coupled or Standalone or there are plans to integrate multiple R/3 backend instances, a * is recommended to denote all categories are designated to the single R/3 backend system.

Define Backend System for Product Category

Transaction: SPRO
Menu Path: Supplier Relationship Management → SRM Server → Technical Basic Settings → Define Backend System for Product Category

Since the backend system must change for each instance, this configuration is not transportable.

Click on the New Entries button.

Specify an asterick for the Category ID field to denote all product
categories and enter in the logical system ID of the backend R/3
system for both the Source System and Target System fields. Since
the categories were replicated from R/3 to EBP, the source and the
target are one in the same.

Determination of Target System using Product Categories			
Category ID	SourceSyst	Tgt system	
*			

Definition of Catalog Call Structures

Catalog call structures must be defined in the EBP system to enable links to display in the Catalog tab of the shopping cart to both internal and external catalogs.

Only internal catalogs will be covered in this chapter

Set Approval Indicator for User ID Requests

Transaction: SPRO

Menu Path: SAP Implementation Guide → Supplier Relationship Management → SRM Server → Master Data → Define External Web Services (Catalogs, Vendor Lists etc.)

Transport: Not Transportable

Click on the New Entries button to create a new Catalog call structure.

In the Web Service ID field, specify a code to identify the type of view that the call structure will represent.

Web Service ID

In the description field, provide a more descriptive name of the view.

Description   IT - Software

In the Business Type field, select "Product Catalog" and leave all other entries as defaulted.

Web Service ID	
Description	IT - Software
Business Type	Product Catalog

Technical settings

☐ Use HTTP GET to Call Web Service

Technical Type of Service	
Logical system	
Path for Symbol for Service	

Click on 🖫 to save the changes.

Leave all entries in the Extended calalog screen as defaulted:

Source of Supply Assigned to Product Catalog

Business partner

Purch. Organization

Additional Functions in SRM Server

☐ Do not Check Product

☐ Display Contract Data in Integrated Catalog

Additional Functions in the Product Catalog

☐ Display Product Data Again in Catalog

☐ Validate Product Data from SAP Enterprise Buyer

☐ Find Supply Sources

☐ Cross-Catalog Search

Technical settings

☐ Use Error Log

☐ Use HTTP GET to Call Web Service

Technical Type of Service

Logical system

Path for Symbol for Service

Click on the ⬅ button and select the line that has the catalog definition that was just generated.

Web Service ID	Description
	IT - Software

Doubleclick on the ☐ Standard Call Structure folder on the left side of the screen.

Click on the New Entries button.

Fill in the appropriate parameters to call the catalog view established in the Requisite environment.

	Parameter Name	Parameter Value	Type
1			URL
2	username		Fixed Value
3	password		Fixed Value
4	HOOK_URL		Return URL
5	~OkCode	ADDI	Fixed Value
6	~target	_top	Fixed Value
7	~caller	CTLG	Fixed Value

Click on the ▣ button to save the catalog parameters.

TIP: For subsequent catalog definitions, use the copy function and change the call structure parameters as necessary.

Define extended attributes

Define extended attributes that typically apply to a large group of users, such as product categories and plants.

Organizational attributes serve many purposes in the EBP system. The primary purpose is to set attributes that define the users experience when shopping. Some example attributes are company codes, plants and cost centers that a user can order against.

This configuration document covers the attributes that will vary per region from a value and assignment perspective, but are required attributes for a user to be able to shop properly. Even with these attributes, the higher they can be assigned in the org structure, the less maintenance over time that will be necessary.

Transaction: PPOMA_BBP
Transport: Not transportable

For our purposes, only a single plant will be defined for all org-based purchases.

Double-Click on the organizational unit that represents a plant or location.

In the window that appears on the bottom of the screen, click on the **Extended Attributes** tab.

Search for the 'System Alias for Accounting System' or 'ACS' attribute in the list.

	Description	Attribute	Exclu	Default	Inherit	Value
	System Alias for Accounting Systems	ACS	☐	☐	☐	

Click on the **⊙ Locations** button to pull up the value fields for plant assignments.

Select from the source system drop-down list the R/3 backend system in which the plant is defined.

Click on the Plant field and launch the field help (F4).

Locate and double-click on the plant which should be adopted.

Click on the Default check box to complete the plant assignment.

Partner ID	Plnt	Comp	Description	Src. System	Default	Deactivate	Inherit
000000				R/3 Backend	☑	☐	

Click on the 🖫 button to save your plant settings.

TIP: If more than one plant should be enabled, add more plants to the list. Only one plant can be assigned the default indicator. If no default value is set, the system will pick the first one it finds as the default.

Maintain Allowable Product Categories (WGR)

Transaction: PPOMA_BBP

Transport Not transportable

The product categories assignment controls which categories users can choose from when creating free text shopping cart line items. Unless there is dire need to restrict which users can order which categories, a wide open range is recommended at the highest level in the org structure to easy maintenance.

Regardless if a full range is enabled at the highest level of the organizational structure, different default values can be established per region. At least one individual entry must be maintained outside of a general range that can be adopted at the system default category. The example below illustrates the creation of a wide open range plus an individual entry that applies to all users.

Double-click on the root purchasing org unit.

Staff assignments (structure)	Code	ID
Corporation		O 5000

Click on the **Extended Attributes** button.

Click on the **◉ Product Categories** radio button if it is not already selected.

Click on the drop-down list of the Src. System field and select the logical system that represents the R/3 backend system in which the product categories were replicated from.

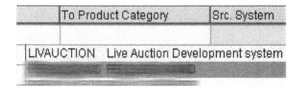

To Product Category	Src. System
LIVAUCTION Live Auction Development system	

Since the category numbers are numeric-based, enter a 0000xxx1 to 9999999999xxx in the Product Category from and To Fields to cover all possible product categories. If certain product categories were replicated by accident or are not intended for immediate use, you may have to list each category out one by one, break up the ranges to skip specific records, or delete the categories using transaction COMM_HIERARCHY.

Product Categories					
Product Category	To Product Category	Src. System	Default	Deactivate	Inhertd
00000000000000000001	99999999999999999999	PIᵣ	☐	☐	☐

Repeat steps 1-3 and this time just put a single value in the Product Category field that will represent the system default.

Click on the Default indicator for the individual line and save your changes.

Product Categories					
Product Category	To Product Category	Src. System	Defsut	Deactivate	Inhertd
00000000000000000001	99999999999999999999		☐	☐	☐
			☑	☐	☐

Assign Purchasing Org and Purchasing Group Specific Attributes

Assign all purchasing organization and purchasing group specific attributes

The purchasing group attributes are essential in defining a smooth sourcing assignment process for the entire buying organization. Once an organizational unit is defined as a purchasing group, this group has no function until it is assigned responsibility for specific product categories and more importantly to a region/group/user.

For our purposes, two purchasing organizations will exist to facilitate all purchases made with the Sodexho and Software Spectrum vendors. A single purchasing organization would not be strategic for the global design where Software Spectrum will serve a broad base of countries across Europe whereas Sodexho will primarily service the UK region.

Building Services: Assigned responsibility to all service related product categories, and assigned organizational responsibility at the United Kingdom Company Code level.

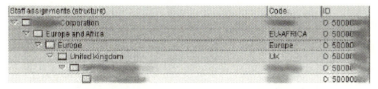

Software: Assigned responsibility to all software related product categories and assigned organizational responsibility at the Europe regional level.

Define Responsibility for Vendor Services

Transaction: PPOMA_BBP
Transport: Not transportable
Double-Click on the purchasing group org unit defined for the Building and Services buying group.

In the window that appears on the bottom of the screen, click on the Responsibility tab.

In the Product Responsible section and product category list line item level, select the backed logical system in which the EBP product categories were replicated from.

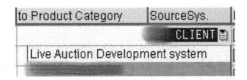

In the Product Category and Product Category To fields, enter in an individual line for each product category that the purchasing group should be responsible for or define ranges that fall within the responsibility of the purchasing group.

Product Responsibility			
Product Category	to Product Category	SourceSys.	D
		CLIENT	☐
		CLIENT	☐
		CLIENT	☐

Click on the ⊞ button to save the new attribute value(s).

Repeat steps 1-5 for each purchasing group.

Assign Responsibility of Purchasing Group to User(s)

Transaction: PPOMA_BBP
Transport: Not transportable

Once the product categories that a buyer is responsible for are defined, a single or multiple assignments need to be made to a place in the org structure or for particular users that this buying group should receive requests from that are placed with the assigned categories.

For Our, only organizational level responsibilities will be defined.

Double-Click on the purchasing group org unit defined for the Building and Services buying group.

| | | United Kingdom | UK | O 500 |
| | | Building and Grounds Services | Service | O 5000 |

In the window that appears on the bottom of the screen, click on the
Responsibility tab.

In the Organizational Responsibility section, type in (or use the
search help) organizational unit number for lines where org level
responsibility should be granted and inherited at all lower levels.

Organizational Responsibility			
O	P	Object ID	Object name
◉	○	5000	United Kingdom

Click on the 💾 button to save the new attribute value.

Repeat steps 1-4 for any additional assignments that should be
made.

Delta Middleware Setup for data transfer from R/3

Once the initial data replication has successfully run for R/3 master data, delta replication requests can be created for manual execution after new master data is generated. For example, if a new product category is created or an existing changed, the delta request should be run to synchronize EBP with the backend R/3 system.

This initial setup of middleware described in this document should only need to be processed in a new SRM client or re-validated when a client copy, system refresh or the existing backend system client is swapped out with a new or other client.

Values set for our purposes (all production PLM-SCM categories blocked for replication)

T023	MATKL Inclusive defined set/array Inequality	(<> Low) 10010
T023	MATKL Inclusive defined set/array Inequality	(<> Low) 10020
T023	MATKL Inclusive defined set/array Inequality	(<> Low) 10030
T023T	MATKL Inclusive defined set/array Inequality	(<> Low) 90000

(You will set your filter values according to your backend requirements.)

Create Request for Delta Product Category Replication

Transaction: R3AR2
Transport: Not Transportable

The following configuration is necessary to replicate updates to existing product categories and the creation of new records into the EBP environment from R/3.

Click on the [✐] button to activate change mode.

Click on the | New Entries | button to begin creating a new entry.

Fill in a short description and select the DNL_CUST_PROD1 customizing object for product categories.

Request Name	ProdCategories
Request header	
Adapter Object	DNL_CUST_PROD1
Object Class	
RequestType	Request: Objects could be loaded from R/3 Backend / CRM DB
☐ Inactive	☐ Use once
Creation Date	
Creation Time	
Creator	

Click on the [💾] button to save the new request.

Click on the [↩] button twice to return to the list of request.

Define Filters for Delta Product Category Request

Transaction: R3AR2

Transport: Not Transportable

Define the filters for product categories to be considered in delta replications.

From the request list, select the product category request that was defined in section A.

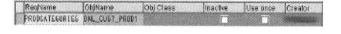

Double click on the ⬜Request detail folder on the left.

Click on the New Entries button to create a product category filter.

Fill T023 for the table name, MATKL for the field name, inclusive, inequality, and insert the value that is to be excluded in the low field. Repeat steps 1-3 for all categories that are to be excluded (once you save the first record, you can use the copy feature to speed up the filter creation process).

Request Name	PRODCATEGORIES

Request detail	
Table Name	T023
Field Name	MATKL
Incl/Excl	Inclusive defined set/array
Option	Inequality (<> Low)
Low	10010
High	
☐ Inactive	

Fill T023T for the table name, MATKL for the field name, inclusive, inequality, and insert the value that is to be excluded in the low field. Repeat steps 1-3 for all categories that are to be excluded.

Request Name	PRODCATEGORIES

Request detail	
Table Name	T023T
Field Name	MATKL
Incl/Excl	Inclusive defined set/array
Option	Inequality (<> Low)
Low	10010
High	
☐ Inactive	

Click on the 💾 button to save the filter settings.

Run Delta Request for Product Category

SAP SRM ADVANCED EBP COOKBOOK

Transaction: R3AR4
Transport: Not Transportable

Run the delta request defined above for product categories.

Enter in or select the request defined in Section A and specify the backend logical system for the Source site and the EBP logical system for the Target Site.

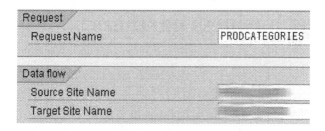

Click on the Enter button to register the Source and Target site names.

Click on the 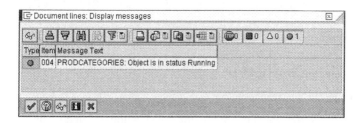 to begin the replication request process.

A pop-up will indicate whether the request process was successfully initiated or not.

Replicate vendors from R/3 to EBP as business partners

Vendor master records must be replicated over to EBP from R/3 before a user can access the vendor from their shopping cart. When in Classic mode, vendor master records remain parent records in the R/3 system; the EBP records simply act as child records. There is some data that can be extended on a vendor master record in the EBP system that the R/3 system either does not replicate over or does not have available, otherwise all other data is overwritten when a subsequent replication is run.

Once a vendor has been replicated over to the EBP system from the R/3 system, all changes to that master record in R/3 can only be synchronized in the EBP system through transaction BBPUPDVD.

Replicate Vendors

Transaction: BBPGETVD

Transport: Not Transportable

You must know which org unit in the organizational structure the vendor master records should be replicated to. In this example, the following org unti was setup in PPOCA_BBP for vendor master records:

Staff assignments (structure)	Code	ID
☐ Supplier Organization	Suppliers	O 500█

Run the BBPGETVD transaction code.

Run the program and select the logical system ID of the R/3 system

Enter in the logical system ID for the backend system where the vendor records are to be replicated from.

Insert the Org Unit ID created in Section A for suppliers in the Object ID field.

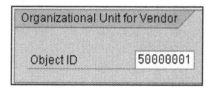

Leave all other fields with their defaulted values.

Scroll down and cick on the

Start Transfer button to begin the

assessment process.

A result screen should display of the number of vendor records possible for replication. Review the list to make sure all of the correct vendor records are being considered.

If you use external number assignment, you will lose some vendors

Number of vendors lost: 2   [Display list]

The following allocation results from the transfer:

Total number of vendors: 3
Adoption of R/3 description: 1   [Display list]
Assignment of internal numbers: 0

[Cancel]   [Back]   [Start transmission]

If the vendor list looks ok, click on the

[Start transmission] to begin the transfer

process.

Enter through the pop-up that appears which notifies that there is an error log to review any issues when transferring vendor records.

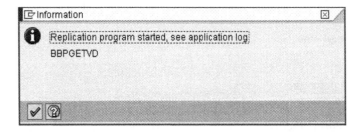

Check transaction SLG1 to make sure no errors occurred.

Ty..	Message Text
△	Error: No Bank Master Data Maintained No Bank Data Transferred
△	Error:
◉	BBPGETVD: Program End Reached

Check transaction PPOSA_BBP to ensure that the vendor records indeed were transferred.

Staff assignments (structure)	Code	ID	Business partn
▽ ☐ Supplier Organization	Suppliers	O	
▽ ☐		O	
☐ 1000000000		O	

Define the Default G/L accounts

Define the default G/L accounts that should be assigned to product category / account assignment combinations.

Transportable as long as logical system is not specified. For the EBP classic scenario, the logical system does not need to be specified.

The EBP system contains the ability to maintain default G/L accounts for line item purchases based on the product category and account assignment type applied to the shopping cart line item. A default G/L account will be proposed for each category / account type used in the sample implementation.

Define G/L Account for Product Category and Account Assignment Category

Transaction: SPRO

Menu Path: Supplier Relationship Management → SRM Server → Cross-Application Basic Settings → Account Assignment → Define G/L Account for Product Category and Account Assignment Category

SAP SRM ADVANCED EBP COOKBOOK

PLEASE NOTE: If the default g/l account configuration needs to be transported, then the search options for categories cannot be used for two reasons:

Categories will not be replicated from R/3 into the EBP gold client

Even if the categories were replicated, selecting the category from a search help will automatically adopt the logical system value.

Click on the New Entries button.

Paste or type in the category number in the Category ID field, the account assignment category (in this example CC represents cost center) in the AccAssCat field and the G/L account in the G/L Account no. field.

Determination of G/L Using Product Categories			
Category ID	SourceSyst	AcctAssCat	G/L account no.

Click on the 💾 button to save the entry(s).

Define purchasing documents to be generated

Define purchasing documents to be generated in R/3 from the EBP shopping cart

In the EBP Classic mode, once a shopping cart is approved, an option exists to either generate a purchase requisition, purchase order or a reservation based on the information available in the shopping cart line items.

There are two ways this configuration can be setup. Each category can be configured separately or a * can be used to denote that all categories follow the same path. Unless there are plans to stray from the Classic EBP mode to De-coupled or Standalone or there are plans to integrate multiple R/3 backend instances, a * is recommended to denote all categories are designated to the single R/3 backend system.

For our purposes, all shopping carts will be setup to create a purchase order unless the data is not complete. If the data is not complete, a purchase requisition will be generated.

SAP SRM ADVANCED EBP COOKBOOK

Define Objects in Backend System (Purch. Reqs, Reservations, Purch. Orders)

Transaction: SPRO

Menu Path: Supplier Relationship Management → SRM Server → Cross-Application Basic Settings → Define Objects in Backend System (Purch. Reqs, Reservations, Purch. Orders)

PLEASE NOTE: asterisks can only be used in either the Purchasing Group or the Category ID field to denote all entries for the object. If a * is entered both fields, the configuration line will not be read for consideration when transferring shopping carts from EBP to R/3.

For Our purposes, since there are more categories than purchasing groups, a * will be used to denote all categories for each given purchasing group.

Click on the **New Entries** button.

Maintain the following entries for each purchasing group defined in the system:

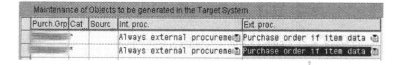

Click on the 🖫 button to save the configuration entries.

Assign all attributes that are typically set at the lower levels of the org structure and probably will vary in settings per region.

Organizational attributes serve many purposes in the EBP system. The primary purpose is to set attributes that define the users experience when shopping. Some example attributes are company codes, plants and cost centers that a user can order against.

This configuration document covers the attributes that will vary per region from a value and assignment perspective, but are required attributes for a user to be able to shop properly. Even with these attributes, the higher they can be assigned in the org structure, the less maintenance over time that will be necessary.

For our purposes, only those attributes relevant to the first facility are set, and are set starting at the Plant level.

Maintain System Alias (ACS)

Transaction: PPOMA_BBP

Transport: Not transportable

Double-Click on the root organizational unit created for purchasing purposes.

In the window that appears on the bottom of the screen, click on the Attributes tab.

Search for the 'System Alias for Accounting System' or 'ACS' attribute in the list.

SAP SRM ADVANCED EBP COOKBOOK

Description	Attribute	Exclu	Default	Inherit	Value
System Alias for Accounting Systems	ACS	☐	☐	☐	

Maintain the logical system for the R/3 system in the Value field.

Description	Attribute	Exclu	Default	Inherit	Value
System Alias for Accounting Systems	ACS	☐	☐	☐	

Click on the 💾 button to save the new attribute value.

Maintain Backend Document Type (BSA)

Transaction: PPOMA_BBP

Transport: Not transportable

The BSA (document type in R/3 system) organizational attribute links an EBP shopping cart to a document type in R/3 for purchase requisitions and purchase orders in R/3. A single document type 'ECPO' should be defined in R/3.This is the value that should be defined for the backend document type preceded by the logical system and a backslash.

With this value set, any requisition or purchase order generated in R/3 from EBP shopping carts will be tied to document type ECPO.

Repeat the steps 1-4 in Section A for the BSA attribute and attribute value.

Description	Attribute	Exclu	Default	Inherit	Value
Document Type in R/3 System	BSA	☐	☐	☐	ECPO

Click on the 💾 button to save the new attribute value.

Maintain Company Code (BUK)

Transaction: PPOMA_BBP

Transport Not transportable

A company code Local definition must be created at the highest level in the org structure where possible shop users may be placed for procurement processes. The BUK (company code) attribute can be set at the lower levels to direct users to more appropriate company code assignments.

In the steps below, a company code is set at the UK level as 1240 for Our. This configuration will probably need to be adjusted as part of the Unit 1 migration with a more appropriate default value.

This Local attribute definition for company code is the key to defining allowable delivery addresses for a given location. In order for users to have the ability to look up addresses from a list, this attribute must be set and the "Edit Internal Addresses" transaction must be used to create the list.

Double-Click on the highest organizational unit that represents a legal entity.

▽ ☐ United Kingdom   UK

Click on the **Function** tab.

Click on the  check box to enable the company code fields to open up.

In the field on the far right with the drop-down list, choose the backend logical system in which the company code is defined.

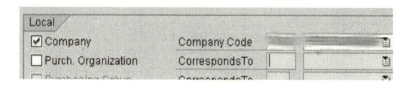

In the company code field, enter the value of the company code that relates to the org unit being maintained.

Local
☑ Company   Company Code
☐ Purch. Organization   CorrespondsTo

Click on the 🔲 button to save the company code definition.

Maintain Movement Type Attribute (BWA)

Transaction: PPOMA_BBP

Transport: Not transportable

The movement type organizational attribute is set with value 201 to handle reservations. Even though reservations are not in scope for the Our implementation, it is necessary to maintain the attribute if the default material group for a given user or site is set to a backend logical system. The EBP system knows that if the user is set for backend procurement, that there might be a possibility for a reservation to be generated, therefore it checks to see that a value for this attribute is maintained. The BWA value should be defined for the as 201 preceeded by the logical system and a backslash.

Repeat the steps 1-4 in Section A for the BWA attribute and attribute value.

	Description	Attribute	Exclu	Default	Inherit	Value
	Movement type	BWA	☐	☐	☐	201

Click on the ▣ button to save the new attribute value.

Local Currency Attribute (CUR)

Transaction: PPOMA_BBP

Transport: Not transportable

The local currency controls what currency the requisitioners see their shopping cart pricing in. If a catalog item is pulled in that is not equal to their local currency attribute, the currency will be converted in the EBP system using the conversion rates replicated over from the R/3 system (which are actually publis hed from the MONEX legacy application). The local currency is an important attribute in driving approval processes to trigger for the local spend and approval limits per region.

Double-Click on the organizational unit created for purchasing purposes for the country where a local currency will need to be defined.

Repeat the steps 2-4 in Section A for the BWA attribute and attribute value. A lookup feature is available on the Value field for this attribute to locate the appropriate currency code.

	Description	Attribute	Exclu	Default	Inherit	Value
	Local Currency	CUR	☐	☐	☐	GBP

Click on the Default check box to ensure that an inherited values are not taken over the lower level defaults.

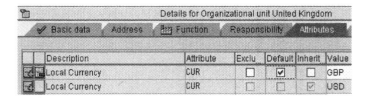

Click on the button to save the new attribute value.

Repeat the steps for each country and also set USD at the root organizational unit to serve as the global operating currency decided upon in the Global S2P design.

		Details for Organizational unit Visteon Corporation

	Basic data	Address	Function	Responsibility	Attributes	E

	Description	Attribute	Exclu	Default	Inherit	Value
	Local Currency	CUR	☐	☐	☐	USD

Maintain Forward Work Item Attribute (FORWARD_WI)

Transaction: PPOMA_BBP

Transport: Not transportable

The forward work item attribute when flagged, automatically sends approval notifications from the user's SAP inbox to their Outlook (or other external) mailbox. According to the Global key decisions defined, this attribute should be set to forward all work items. The exclusion checkbox can be used to stop the forwarding if necessary for a given user or group of users.

Repeat the steps 1-4 in Section A for the FORWARD_WI attribute and attribute value.

	Description	Attribute	Exclu	Default	Inherit	Value
	Flag: Forward Work Item	FORWARD_WI	☐	☐	☐	X

Click on the ▣ button to save the new attribute value.

Maintain Current ITS of User (ITS_DEST)

Transaction: PPOMA_BBP

Transport: Not transportable

The ITS_DEST attribute is used to build the URL to go into the emails to approvers that they can click to launch the SRM application to review the approval item. This attribute will be set with the ITS for the EBP system for Our, but will need to be revisited with the Enterprise Portals application is rolled out in Unit

Repeat the steps 1-4 in Section A for the ITS_DEST attribute and attribute value.

	Description	Atribute	Exclu	Defaut	inhent	Value
	Current ITS of User	ITS_DEST				

Click on the 🖫 button to save the new attribute value.

Maintain Account Assignment Categories (KNT)

Transaction: PPOMA_BBP

Transport Not transportable

The account assignment categories that a user is able to order against is maintained with the KNT attribute. At a minimum, cost center purchasing will be enabled for all users. The attribute therefore for Our is setup at the root organzational level.

Repeat the steps 1-3 in Section A for the KNT attribute and attribute value.

In the KNT value field, either click on the search help button or hit F4 to look at the list of possible values.

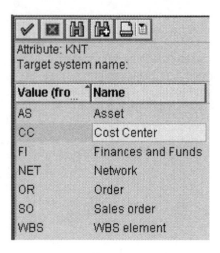

Double-click on the Cost Center account assignment entry to adopt this value.

	Description	Attribute	Exclu	Default	Inherit	Value
	Account assignment category	KNT	☐	☐	☐	CC

Click on the ▣ button to save the new attribute value.

Maintain System Alias Attribute (SYS)

Transaction: PPOMA_BBP

Transport: Not transportable

The SYS (system alias) organizational attribute controls the list displays in the central invoice and goods receipt transactions for a particular system. If a system value is not set for this attribute, the records for that system will not be displayed for the users within these transactions. For example, if an R/3 PO is created and the logical system for that Purchase Order is not configured with the

SYS attribute, the user will not see his/her PO in the goods receipt transaction and therefore cannot post a goods issue. The attribute is maintained at the root level in the organizational structure because all EBP users will be posting purchase order and goods receipts to a single backend R/3 system.

Repeat the steps 1-4 in Section A for the ACS attribute and attribute value.

	Description	Attribute	Exclu.	Default	Inherit	Value
	System Alias	SYS	☐	☐	☐	

Click on the 💾 button to save the new attribute value.

Maintain Systems for Vendor Master Records (VENDOR_ACS, VENDOR_SYS)

Transaction: PPOMA_BBP

Transport: Not transportable

Similar to the ACS accounting system reference attribute, the vendor_acs and vendor_sys attributes are used to determine which system to validate vendor accouting for and vendor master records. Since all vendor data will be resident in the R/3 backend system, both attributes should be set to the logical system of the backend system client in which the vendor master records will be or are replicated from.

Repeat the steps 1-4 in Section A for the SYS attribute and attribute value.

	Description	Attribute	Exclu	Default	Inherit	Value
	Accounting System for Vendor	VENDOR_ACS	☐	☐	☐	
	System Alias for Vendor	VENDOR_SYS	☐	☐	☐	

Click on the 🖫 button to save the new attribute value.

Maintain Allowable Catalogs (CAT)

Transaction: PPOMA_BBP
Transport: Not transportable

Catalog views are assigned to the users through the CAT organizational attribute. This attribute value is case-sensitive, ensure the catalog ID is entered as it is configured in the system.

Repeat the steps 1-4 in Section A for the CAT attribute and attribute value.

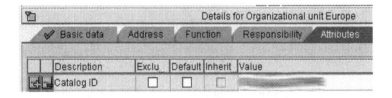

	Description	Exclu	Default	Inherit	Value
	Catalog ID	☐	☐	☐	

Details for Organizational unit Europe
✓ Basic data | Address | Function | Responsibility | Attributes

Click on the 🖫 button to save the new attribute value.

Setup of ALE in the EBP system for Goods Receipt processing between EBP and R/3

The following configuration covers all of the steps to enable goods receipt transfer to R/3 from EBP. Unlike most other EBP to R/3 communication, receipts and invoices use IDOC for document transfer because receipt transfer does not require real time response as a requisition or purchase order does. In the future, this document transfer process will be converted over to XI.

In the event that invoice entry is enabled in the SRM system in the future, the additional message types for invoice entry must be setup and transferred over to the R/3 system. For our implementation, only the goods receipt message types were maintained.

Create Model for R/3 Backend

Transaction: SPRO (or BD64)

IMG Location: Supplier Relationship Management → SRM Server → Technical Basic Settings → ALE Settings (Logical System) → Distribution (ALE) → Modeling and Implementing Business Processes → Maintain Distribution Model and Distribute Views

Transport: **Not Transportable**

Click on the [☐ Create model view] button.

Fill in the Short Text and Technical Name fields and click on the green check mark.

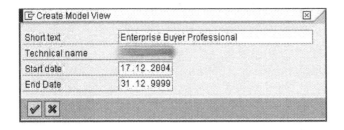

Add Goods Receipt Message Types

Transaction: BD64

IMG Location: Supplier Relationship Management → SRM Server → Technical Basic Settings → ALE Settings (Logical System) → Distribution (ALE) → Modeling and Implementing Business Processes → Maintain Distribution Model and Distribute Views

Transport: Not transportable

Goods receipts entered in EBP are transferred to R/3 via the
MBGMCR and ACC_GOODS_MOVEMENT message types.

Click on the 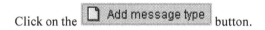 button.

Fill in the EBP logical system ID in the Sender field, the R/3 logical
system ID in the Receiver field and MBGMCR in the Message
Type field and click on the green check mark to commit the entry.

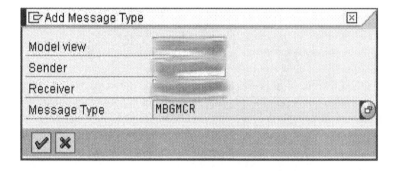

Repeat step two with the ACC_GOODS_MOVEMENT message
type.

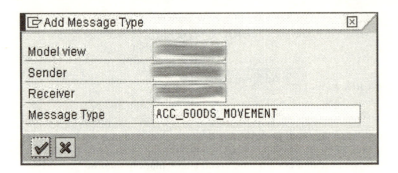

Click on the 💾 button to save the model view.

Generate Partner Profiles

Transaction: BD64

Menu Path: Environment → Generate partner profiles

Transport: Not Transportable

Once all of the message types are added to the EBP model, the partner profiles must be generated before the model is distributed to the R/3 system for usage.

Prior to generating the Partner Profiles, the Model view must be saved. Click on the Save button from the Model View screen if not already done.

Execute the Generate Partner Profiles report from the menu path specified above.

Make sure the model name used in step A is filled in the Model
View field.

In the Partner System field, enter the logical system ID for the EBP
system as well as the R/3 system.

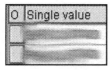

Make sure the "Transfer IDoc Immediately" and "Trigger
Immediately" radio buttons are selected.

Model View		to	
Partner System		to	
Check Run	☐		

Default Parameters for Partner Profile

Postprocessing: Authorized Users

Ty.	US User
ID	

Outb. Parameters

Version	3 IDoc record types from Version 4.0 onwards
Pack Size	100 IDocs

Output Mode

◉ Transfer IDoc immediately

○ Collect IDocs and transfer

Inb. Parameters

Processing

◉ Trigger immediately

○ Trigger by background program

Click on the ⊕ button to generate the profiles.

The output for the report should look similar to the following:

Distribute the Model to R/3

Transaction: BD64

Menu Path: Edit → Model view → Distribute

Transport: Not Transportable

The model must be distributed to the R/3 system in order for the IDoc transfer process to be possible.

Click on the EBP model view that is to be distributed to R/3.

Execute the following menu path:

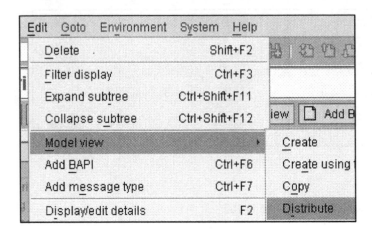

Select the Logical System ID of the backend system where the model is to be distributed from and click on the green check mark to execute.

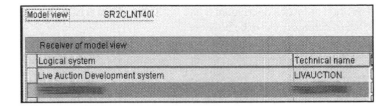

Make sure you received a successful message:

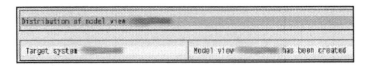

Automate Vendor Replication

Establish an automated process for replicating updating vendors

In the EBP system, an automated vendor replication and update job can be activated to eliminate the need to periodically manually retrieve new vendor master records or vendor master record updates. This configuration document covers the process of automating the creation and update of records.

Configure Automated Vendor Replication

IMG Menu Path: SAP Implementation Guide → Supplier Relationship Management → SRM Server → Technical Basic Settings → Settings for Vendor Synchronization → Make Global Settings
Transport: Not Transportable

Click on the New Entries button.

Check the both check boxes to make sure new records are transferred and duplicate records are not transferred.

☑ Create New Vendors Also

If vendors are to be created also, check the following details
☑ Carry Out Address Comparison to Determine Duplicates

126

Enter in the org unit number from the Organizational structure designated for supplier master records.

Organizational Unit in EBP for the Vendor   50000001

Select "Only Assign R/3 Numbers" from the vendor number assignment drop-down list.

Vendor Number Assignment Type   Only Assign R/3 Numbers

Maintain an email address as the contact person for the company code.

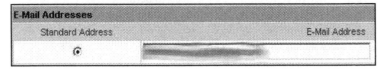

Click on the 🔲 button to save the record.

Configure Backend Specific Vendor Replication Settings

IMG Menu Path: SAP Implementation Guide → Supplier Relationship Management → SRM Server → Technical Basic Settings → Settings for Vendor Synchronization → Define Settings for Each Backend System

Transport: Not Transportable

Click on the New Entries button.

Put 0001 in the Order field to put the first entry as the first priority, enter in the logical sytem ID of the backend system the vendor records are to be replicated from and check the LFURL as email box so the email address on the vendor master records are transferred automatically to the EBP system.

Click on the ⊞ button to save the entry.

Setup for Shopping Cart Status Jobs

Setup EBP jobs to exchange documents status between EBP and the R/3 backend system.

EBP sends all data to the R/3 system real-time via RFC's or through IDOC's. When data is changed in R/3 however, the EBP system is not updated in real-time, instead via batch jobs. This data is updated in EBP in order to provide accurate order status for the users operating in the EBP environment and to allow the creation of follow-on documents in EBP such as goods receipts and invoices. Two jobs are available in the EBP system to update this status information and should be setup to run on fairly regular intervals.

CLEANER JOB: The cleaner job was created by SAP to delete unnecessary (obsolete) data/records in the EBP system after verification that all order data was successfully posted in the R/3 system. For example, when a purchase order is successfully posted in R/3, the cleaner job will delete temporary shopping cart table records that are no longer necessary in EBP since the master record of the order shifts to the R/3 system in de-coupled mode.

STATUS JOB: The status job was created by SAP to update the EBP system with data such as purchase requisition number, purchase order number, goods received or invoices recorded manually in R/3, etc. The report should not be run on a frequent basis at short intervals unless the order count from EBP to R/3 is not that high. Otherwise, a recommended interval for running the report is approximately every hour. Until this job runs, the user will not see the number of the backend document created in R/3 for a particular shopping cart in the history tab of the check status transaction.

The CLEAN_REQREQ_UP and BBP_GET_STATUS2 jobs will be configured to run in each EBP client to synchronize status data between EBP and R/3. The following are recommended intervals will be setup within the respective EBP clients. These values are subject to change over time if performance becomes an issue or the intervals are set too far apart and performance has not been an issue.

System	Job	Interval (in minutes)
Sandbox	Cleaner	1
	Status	3
Development	Cleaner	1
	Status	5
Quality Assurance	Cleaner	1
	Status	30/10
Production	Cleaner	1
	Status	60

Set Control Parameters

Transaction: SPRO

Menu Path: Supplier Relationship Management → SRM Server → Technical Basic Settings → Set Control Parameters

For the SPOOL_JOB_USER control record, enter in the System user created by the Basis team to run jobs.

Key control record	ConfigurationKeyDescri	Value control record
SPOOL_JOB_USER	User that execueds spool job.	EBP_JOB

Create a new entry for the CLEANER_JOB.

Key control record	ConfigurationKeyDescri	Value control record
CLEANER_USER	User to run cleaner job	EBP_JOB

Create a new entry to define the frequency at which the CLEANER_JOB should be run. ENSURE THIS SETTING IS ADJUSTED PROPERLY IN EACH ENVIRONMENT!!

Key control record	ConfigurationKeyDescri	Value control record
CLEANER_INTERVAL	Frequency of R/3 Status Job	1

Click on 🖫 to save the changes.

Schedule R/3 Status Update Job

Transaction: SM36
Report: BBP_GET_STATUS_2
Transport: Not Transportable (will be setup on auto schedule software)

The get status report updates the user shopping cart history screen with the follow-on documents created in the R/3 system from shopping carts such as reservations, purchase orders, requisitions, goods receipts, etc. In the development system, this job should be run at a high frequency for testing purposes. In the production system this report should only run a few times a day, maximum every hour unless frequent archiving is done for checking purchase history.

Enter the name of the report in the Job Name Field

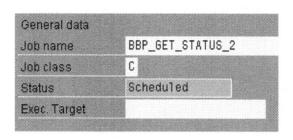

General data	
Job name	BBP_GET_STATUS_2
Job class	C
Status	Scheduled
Exec. Target	

Click on the **Start condition** button to set the intervals in which the job should run.

Click on the **Immediate** button to denote an immediate start time.

Click on the **Period values** button to specify run time intervals.

Click on the **Other period** button and specify the appropriate interval for the system and client referenced in the table in Section 2 above.

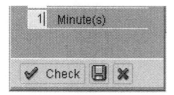

Click on the button 3 times to save the start condition variables set.

Click on the **Step** button to specify which report to run.

In the User field, enter in the name of the Job User that has SAP_ALL access and is setup as a system user.

Click on the ABAP program button to enter in the program name.

Maintain the following ABAP Program values:

ABAP program	
Name	BBP_GET_STATUS_2
Variant	
Language	EN

Click on the 💾 button to save the Program variables set.

Click on the 💾 button to save the job.

Verify that a successful message was issued after the save.

✓ Job BBP_GET_STATUS_2 saved with status: Released

Run Cleaner Job

Transaction: SA38

Report: START_CLEANER

Transport: Not Transportable

The cleaner job cleans up entries in the EBP tables after receiving
updated status' through the BBP_GET_STATUS_2 job. The steps
in Section A must be completed prior to starting the cleaner job as
this job uses the System user setup in Section A to run the report.

Enter in the START_CLEANER report name in the Program field.

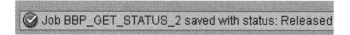

Program	START_CLEANER

Click on the Execute to start the cleaner report. Once executed, the system will automatically schedule the job CLEAN_REQREQ_UP which runs at a 3-5 minute variable depending on the system configuration. If this job is ever stopped by the system, it must be rescheduled through the START_CLEANER report.

Activate workflow for user creation

Activate workflow for user creation to eliminate the possibility for a user to acquire a user account automatically when the Register link is clicked on the logon screen.

The approval indicator for user creation controls whether or not a workflow should be triggered when a user puts in a request for a user ID using the Register User ID link the SRM logon screen.

This link will not be an issue when SRM is rolled out in the Enterprise Portals application. This example assumes that users will log directly into the SRM application to request and process shopping carts.

The indicator will be set for our implementation to ensure that the request fails in the event a user tries to process a Request for a User ID.

___

Set Approval Indicator for User ID Requests

Transaction: SPRO
Menu Path: Supplier Relationship Management → SRM Server →
Master Data → Create Users → Set Approval Indicator
Transport: Not Transportable

Click on the checkbox to activate approvals for user ID requests.

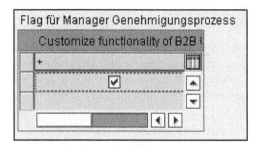

Click on ⬛ to save the changes.

Create standard and alternative approved ship-to list.

Ship-to addresses in the EBP system are maintained at the
Company Code level. A standard address is maintained that acts as
the default address for all user purchases which are assigned that
particular company code. Additional addresses can be maintained
that the user can choose from.

This implementation will have a default standard address
maintained as well as additional facility specific approved addresses
to represent all of the satellite ship-to locations.

Note: A user must have access to transaction code
BBPADDRINTC to create/change/display ship-to addresses.

Create Standard Address for Company Code

SRM Menu Option: Edit Internal Addresses

Role: Buyer

The following steps should be used to create a standard address at the company code level.

On the Business Partner Overview, click the 🔍 button to create a standard address for the given company code line in which the address should be defined.

Click on the Display / Change button to enter into change mode.

Click on the Ship-to Address and Copy as Default checkboxes to establish the company code as the standard default address for all purchases made against that particular company code.

At minimum, maintain all required fields (denoted by a red astericks) within the address section:

Maintain an email address as the contact person for the company code.

In the communications protocol section, a Standard Communications Protocol value is mandatory. Choose the option for Send via Email.

Click on the [Save Address] button to save the standard address.

Create Additional Ship-to's Per Company Code

SRM Menu Option: Edit Internal Addresses

Our Role: Buyer

The following steps should be used to create additional ship-to addresses at the company code level.

On the Business Partner Overview, click on the button to create a standard address for the given company code line in which the address should be defined.

Click on the Ship-to Address checkbox to denote that this is an a ship-to address definition.

At minimum, maintain all required fields (denoted by a red astericks) within the address section:

* Maintain an email address as the contact person for the company code ship-to address.

In the communications protocol section, a Standard Communications Protocol value is mandatory. Choose the option for Send via Email.

FTP Address	
HTTP Address	
Standard Communications Protocol *	Send via E-mail ▼

Click on the Save Address button to save the standard address.

Repeat steps 1-6 for each additional address.

Activate vendor list

Activate vendor list functionality to enable automatic sourcing.

Activating the vendor list allows the buying organization to use Vendor Lists to auto-source all catalog and non-catalog shopping cart line items based on purchasing organization and product category.

Set Approval Indicator for User ID Requests

Transaction: SPRO

Menu Path: SAP Implementation Guide → Supplier Relationship Management → SRM Server → Sourcing → Define Sourcing via Vendor List Only

Click on the checkbox to activate the source lists:

Source of Supply Determination via Vendor List Only

☑ Source of supply determination exclusively via AVL is active

Click on to save the changes.

Activate application monitors

Activate application monitors to track and react to any errors in the EBP system.

The application monitors must be activated in order to receive errors into the queues and react to them. This configuration step should only need to be performed when a new client is established or after a client refresh.

Transaction: SPRO

Menu Path: SAP Implementation Guide → Supplier Relationship Management → SRM Server → Cross-Application Basic Settings → Start Application Monitors

Transport: Not Transportable

Click on the following IMG activity.

Ensure a successful message was posted:

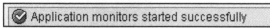

JIM STEWART

Change the tax calculation to "No Tax Calculation"

The EBP system allows several avenues for calculating tax for shopping cart line items.

For our purposes, no taxes will be calculated for shopping cart line items.

Set No Calculation of Taxes

Transaction: SPRO

Menu Path: SAP Implementation Guide → Supplier Relationship Management → SRM Server → Cross-Application Basic Settings → Tax Calculation → Determine System for Tax Calculation

Select the radio button for "No Tax Calculation":

Defining System for Tax Calculation		
System for tax calculation		Choose
No Tax Calculation	🔽	⦿

Click on the 💾 button to save the configuration.

JIM STEWART

Set "general task" for approval tasks

The standard workflows delivered by the system all have the "No general task" setting applied. Unless roles are attached to the workflow to determine who can and cannot process a particular workflow, then no one can process the workflow. Therefore the Workflow Templates should be converted to "General Task" so they can be used. Individual approval tasks may or may not be set with "General Task".

This is a one time configuration step for each time a new EBP instance is implemented (i.e., QA, PRD, BUS Sim, etc).

Our implementation will require a general task setting on the Goods Receipt workflow (10400010) as well as the shopping cart approvals workflow.

Mark Workflow Templates as General Tasks

Transaction: PFTC_CHG

Menu Path: Additional Data → Agent assignment → Maintain

Refer to the following steps to manually set the General Task status for approval tasks.

Choose Task Type "Workflow Template" and enter in the appropriate workflow template number in the Task Number field.

Task type	Workflow Template
Task	10400010 NoApprovCF
Name	Goods Receipt Workflow Without Approval

Go to the Maintain Agent assignment screen via the menu path above

Put the cursor on the Workflow Template number and click on the Attributes... button.

Change the status from "No general task" to "General task".

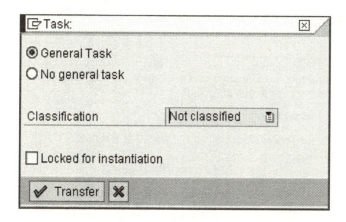

Repeat for each Workflow Template that will be used for approvals.

Define the start conditions for shopping cart approvals and workflow with no approval for goods receipts.

Create vendor source lists for each product category. Vendor lists allow automatic sourcing on.

Vendor Master Records and product categories must be defined and the org structure must be nearly complete before performing the configuration steps in this document.

Create a Vendor List

Transaction: Process Vendor List (BBPALVMAINT)
Role: Purchaser

Select Vendor list, the appropriate Purchasing Organization and Product Category.

Process Vendor List

Create Vendor List

Vendor List Type	Vendor List ▼
Purchasing Organization	▼
Product Category	🔍
Product	🔍

Click on the Create button.

Click on the 🔍 at the line item level to begin locating a supplier (vendor) that should be preferred or non-preferred for the particular commodity.

Conduct a search for the appropriate vendor and click on the link for the supplier that should be sourced.

Search Result: 1 Entry	
Name org.	City
Software Spectrum	High Wycombe

Select whether the vendor should be preferred (active) or non-preferred (inactive).

Sources of Supply			
Item	Active	Inactv.	Vendor
1	⦿	○	1000000000
2	⦿	○	

Specify a descriptive name for the vendor list that describes its origin and nature.

General Data	
Description	EU-BusFuncSoftware
Vendor List	0000000002

Click on the ▢Release button to save and release the source list.

Note: Ensure the status was adjusted appropriately

Status	Released

R3 Configuration

The following configuration needs to be completed on the "backend" or "R3" system.

Create Plans and Make Assignments

Create Plant and make assignments to Purchasing Organizations

As described in Configuration Document 01- Define Purchasing Organization Hierarchy, a purchasing organization is assigned to a plant or plants for which it is responsible for all purchasing activities. Once a Purchasing Organization has been created, the Plants for which it is responsible must also be created.

For our purposes, the PLM/SCM Plant naming convention for the SAP environment will be adopted. The PLM/SCM would be configured all SAP plants for your company's manufacturing sites.

The Plant number Ranges will be defined as follows :

Where:

Plants will fall within the range: 1001 – 8999

This could be further defined as:

North American Plants	1000 – 1999
Europe and Africa Plants	2000 – 2999
Asia Plants	3000 – 3999
South American Plants	4000 - 4999

Create Plant

Transaction: SPRO

Program/Method/IMG Location: IMG > Enterprise Structure >
Definition > Logistics – General > Define, copy, delete, check Plant

The Plant must be defined with the characteristics particular to that
Plant. This includes: SAP Plant Code (according to PLM/SCM
naming convention); Plant description, Detailed Information of the
Plant and the physical address of the Plant.

Click on the 'Define Plant' option and select .

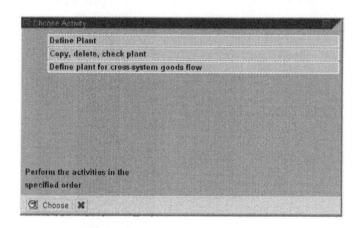

Select the **New Entries** button.

Enter Plant details as follows:

Plant	2063
Name 1	Visteon VCTC Basildon
Name 2	

Detailed information

Language Key	
House No. and Street	
PO Box	
Postal Code	
City	
Country Key	
Region	
County code	
City code	
Jurisdiction Code	
Factory calendar	

Select the ▣ button to add address details of the Plant. This is the physical address that will be referenced for all transactions processed against this Plant in the SAP application.

Enter the address details as required.

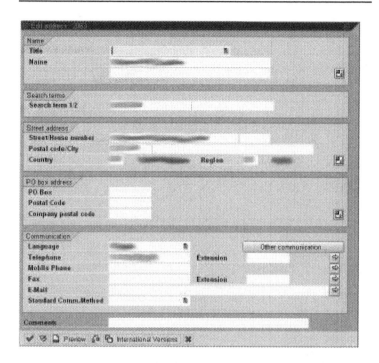

If additional Address or Communication details are required, select the ⬛ icon. Once all the Address and Communication details have been entered, select the ✔ icon.

Select the 💾 button to Save the Plant details.

Assign Purchasing Organization to Plant

Transaction: OX17

Img Location: IMG > Enterprise Structure > Assignment > Materials Management > Assign Purchasing Organization to Plant

Assignment of the Plant to Purchasing Organisation occurs to enable procurement activities to be undertaken for that Plant/ Purchasing Organisation relationship.

Select the Purchasing Organisation to be assigned.

Select the **Assign** button.

Select the Plant to be assigned and select the check icon.

Select the button.

Select the button to save the assignment.

Create a Storage Location within a Plant

Transaction: OX17

Program/Method/IMG Location: IMG > Enterprise Structure > Assignment > Materials Management > Assign Purchasing Organization to Plant

A Storage Location is a further logistical sub-division of a Plant. A Storage Location is used to hold stock within a plant and therefore, is required for receiving and issuing stock that is held in inventory. A Storage Location may also be used for retieving incoming goods addresses for vendor deliveries.

Enter the Plant for which the Storage Location should be created.

Click on .

Click on New Entries.

Enter the four-digit SAP Storage Location Code and a description of the Storage Location.

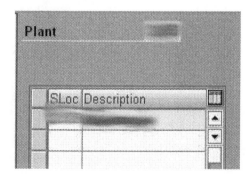

Click on [📷] to save the creation and assignment.

To enter address details of the Storage Location, select the line item of the relevant Storage Location and double click on the 'Address of Storage Locations' line on the left pane.

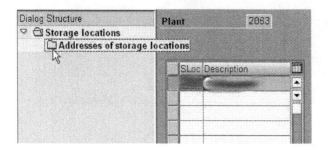

Click on the icon to add an address number.

Enter the Storage Location address reference number and enter.

Define Purchasing Organization Hierarchy

The Purchasing Organization hierarchy comprises Company Codes, Purchasing Organizations, Plants and Purchasing Groups.

A **Company Code** is its own legal entity within SAP with its own Balance Sheet and Profit and Loss account and forms part of the your Corporate Group.

A **Purchasing Organization** is the organizational unit within a business that is responsible for the procurement of goods and services for plants that fall within a particular region. The Purchasing Organization also negotiates terms and conditions of contracts and purchases from vendors and assumes legal responsibility for these purchases for the Plants that the Purchasing Organization is responsible for. The Plants that a Purchasing Organization is responsible for is dependant on its assignment in SAP and is described in Configuration Document 02- Setup Purchasing Assignments.

A **Plant** is an operational unit within an organization and has its own address, language, country and master data. A Plant is assigned to Purchasing Organization in the Implementation Guide (IMG) and the Purchasing Organization then assumes the roles and activities involved in the procurement of goods and services described above for that Plant.

Purchasing Groups are further sub-divisions of the Purchasing Organization and are responsible for the day-to-day buying activities. Typically a Purchasing Group can be seen as a single buyer or group of buyers responsible for purchasing activities. A Purchasing Group is not assigned to a single Purchasing Organization or Plant and is able to carry out buying activities across these structures.

A single Purchasing Organization will be created in our example. This Purchasing Organization will be responsible for the purchasing activities described above for the Plants included in our implementation. The Purchasing Organization created for Our will be a European Purchasing Organization and its responsibilities will be extended to include further Plants and Company Codes in Europe for Segments 1 and 2 of the Global implementation.

Create Purchasing Organization

Transaction: SPRO

IMG Location: IMG > Enterprise Structure > Definition > Materials Management > Maintain Purchasing Organization

Create entries for the Purchasing Organisations that are to be created for the organisation.

Choose New Entries to add a Purchasing Organization.

Enter the SAP Purchasing Organization Code and a description of the Purchasing Organization:

Select .

Create Purchasing Groups

Transaction: SPRO

IMG Location: IMG > Materials Management > Purchasing > Create Purchasing Groups

Create entries for the Purchasing Groups that are to created for the Purchasing activities.

Choose New Entries to add a Purchasing Group.

Enter the SAP Purchasing Group Code, description of the Purchasing Group and any contact details that may be relevant:

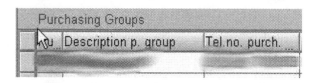

Select 💾.

Enter the address details of the Storage Location and select the ✅ icon.

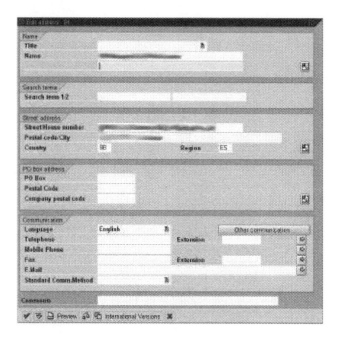

Select the 💾 to save the Storage Location and Storage Location details.

Define Number Ranges for R/3 Purchasing Documents

Number Ranges need to be created for SAP R/3 documents that will be created or interfaced from the EBP system. When a Purchase Requisition is created and interfaced back down to the SAP R/3 system, a number range should exist in R/3 such that the next available number in that range will be used to reference that Purchase Requisition. The Purchase Requisition number range for requisitions coming from the EBP front-end should be the same in both the SAP R/3 system and the SAP R/3 back-end system. The configuration of Purchase Requisition number ranges is covered in configuration document – "01 - EBP Number Ranges ".

Number ranges can be transported in SAP by using the menu option rather than the standard SAP configuration transport method. Select Interval > Transport to transport the number range between clients. **This however, deletes the number range in the source client.** As a general rule it is recommended that ALL Purchasing number ranges be manually entered into the SAP clients in which they are required.

Maintain Purchasing Requisition Number Ranges

Transaction: OMH7

IMG Location: IMG > Materials Management > Purchasing >
Purchase Requisition > Define Number Ranges

No	From Number	To Number
01	0010000000	0019999999
02	0090000000	0099999999
03	2000000000	2999999999
04	3000000000	3999999999

Choose [✎ Intervals] to maintain number ranges.

Click on [Interval] to maintain or create a new number range.

Enter the Purchase Requisition number range.

Select the [💾] icon.

Maintain Purchasing Order Number Ranges

Transaction: OMH6

IMG Location: IMG > Materials Management > Purchasing > Purchase Order > Define Number Ranges

The following Number ranges should be configured:

No	From Number	To Number	Current Number	Ext. Number Range
41	4100000000	4199999999		X
44	4400000000	4499999999		X
45	4500000000	4599999999		
46	4600000000	4699999999		
60	6000000000	6099999999		
61	6100000000	6199999999		X

Choose  to maintain number ranges.

Click on ![Interval] to maintain or create a new number range.

Enter the Purchase Requisition number range.

Select the ![icon] icon

Create Number Ranges for Vendor Accounts

Transaction: XKN1

IMG Location: IMG > Financial Accounting > Accounts Receivable and Accounts Payable > Vendor Accounts > Master Data > Preparation for creating Vendor Master Data > Create Number Ranges for Vendor Accounts

The following Number ranges should be configured:

No	From Number	To Number	Current Number	Ext. Number Range
01	0000000001	0000099999		
02	0000100000	0000199999		
XX	A	ZZZZZZZZZZ		X
Z1	1000000000	1099999999		

Choose [🖉 Intervals] to maintain number ranges.

Click on [Interval] to maintain or create a new number range.

Enter the Purchase Requisition number range.

Select the [💾] icon

Middleware Setup

The middleware component is configured to make certain kinds of data transfer possible in the EBP system.

Middleware is used on the R/3 application to transfer and synchronize master data between other SAP instances such as Enterprise Buyer Professional and Supplier Self Services. Example master data includes plants, commodity codes, material master records, etc.

This initial setup of middleware described in this document should only need to be processed in a new SRM client or re-validated when a client copy, system refresh or the existing backend system client is swapped out with a new or other client.

Create Consumer type EBP

Transaction: SM30

Table: CRMCONSUM

A logical system definition referring to the EBP-SRM system is necessary so the backend system knows where to respond to for synchronization requests. Create a new entry for user EBP and make sure the Active checkbox is marked.

Possible Users of R/3 Adapter Functionality			
User	Ac	Description	Q_Prefix
EBP	✓	Enterprise Buyer Professional	R3A

Define Customizing Objects for EBP Consumer

Transaction: SM30

Table: CRMSUBTAB

Customizing objects must be defined for the EBP consumer to match the objects resident in the EBP system. Copy the CRM (MATERIAL, CUSTOMIZING and SERVICE_MASTER) records from the table and change the consumer type to EBP for the new entries.

MATERIAL

User	EBP
Objectn.Downl.	
Up or Download	Download
Obj.Class	MATERIAL
Function	
Object Type	

Subscription Table for Up and Download Objects	
Function Module	CRS_MATERIAL_EXTRACT
☐ Inactive	

CUSTOMIZING

User	EBP
Objectn.Downl.	
Up or Download	Download
Obj.Class	CUSTOMIZING
Function	
Object Type	

Subscription Table for Up and Download Objects	
Function Module	CRS_CUSTOMIZING_EXTRACT
☐ Inactive	

SERVICE_MASTER

User	EBP
Objectn.Downl.	
Up or Download	Download
Obj.Class	SERVICE_MASTER
Function	
Object Type	

Subscription Table for Up and Download Objects	
Function Module	CRS_SERVICE_EXTRACT
☐ Inactive	

Define Logical System for Initial Downloads

Transaction: SM30
Table: CRMRFCPAR
Transport: Not Transportable

Create entries in table CRMRFCPAR in the backend R/3 system for initial and delta downloads using the logical system name of the EBP client in which replication exchange will take place. These entries must be manually created in each new EBP client connected to an R/3 backend system, as the correct logical system must be populated in the Destination field.

Initial Download Definition

User	EBP
Object Name	*
Destination	
Load Type	Initial Download

Definitions for RFC Connections	
Out Queue Name	
In Queue Name	
BAPINAME	
INFO	
InQueue Flag	X
Send XML	Send XML
☐ Stop Data	
☐ Discard Data	
☐ Data Rcd Inactive	

Material Delta Definition

User	EBP
Object Name	MATERIAL
Destination	
Load Type	Delta Download

Definitions for RFC Connections

Out Queue Name	
In Queue Name	
BAPINAME	
INFO	
InQueue Flag	X
Send XML	Send XML
☐ Stop Data	
☐ Discard Data	
☐ Data Rcd Inactive	

On Request Download Definition

User	EBP
Object Name	*
Destination	
Load Type	Request

Definitions for RFC Connections	
Out Queue Name	
In Queue Name	
BAPINAME	
INFO	
InQueue Flag	X
Send XML	Send XML
☐ Stop Data	
☐ Discard Data	
☐ Data Rcd Inactive	

Create Active Entry for MATERIAL Customizing Object

Transaction: SM30

Table: CRMPAROLTP

Create an entry in table CRMPAROLTP in the backend R/3 system to active filtering for the download of materials. This will help make the material replication process run more efficiently.

Parameter name	CRM_FILTERING_ACTIVE
Param. Name 2	MATERIAL
Param. Name 3	
User	EBP
Param.Value	X
Param. Value 2	

Define Purchase Document Types

SAP uses Document Types to group documents with similar characteristics together. **Purchase Requisitions** are grouped together depending on, firstly, where they originate from and secondly, by what type of purchasing document they will become. The number range is assigned to that particular document type enabling SAP to create Purchase Requisitions from a particular Number Range. All requisitions will be generated from the Enterprise Buyer Professional front-end, therefore a new document type has to be configured and the number range assigned to this Document Type in the SAP R/3 system has to agree with the number range for Purchase Requisitions in the SRM system.

Purchase Orders are similarly grouped together by document type depending on the PO characteristics. PO's for the S2P project will be initiated from the EBP front-end and as such all PO's will have the item category ECPO.

For the S2P project the Document Type ECPO is linked to relevant Purchasing Item Categories and assigned the correct number range. In the case of Purchase Requisitions, this number range should be identical to the EBP Shopping Cart Number Range.

Define Document Types for Purchase Requisitions

Transaction: SPRO

IMG Location: IMG > Materials Management > Purchasing >
Purchase Requisition > Define Document Types

Type	Doc. type descript.	Item i	NR int. as	No. rng. ext	Field sel.	Contr	OverR	Variant
ECPO	EBP Purchase Req.	10	01	02	NBB		☑	
FO	Framework requisn.	10	01	02	FOF		☐	SRV
NB	Purchase requisition	10	01	02	NBB		☐	
RV	Outl. agmt. requisn.	10	01	02	RVB	R	☐	

Select **New Entries**.

Enter the new Document type, Description of the Document Type,
item indicator, internal number range number, external number
range number and field selection key

Type	Doc. type descript.	Item i	NR int. as	No. rng. ext	No. rng.ALE	Updat	Field sel.	Co
DB	Dummy purchase order	10	45	41		SAP	NBF	
ECPO	EBP Standard PO	10	45	44		SAP	NBF	
FO	Framework order	10	45	41		SAP	FOF	
NB	Standard PO	10	45	41		SAP	NBF	
UB	Stock transport ord.	10	45	41		SAP	UBF	T

Select the 🖫 icon.

To assign the relevant Item Categories, select the document type
created and double click on "ALLOWED ITEM CATEGORIES"
on the Dialog Structure.

Dialog Structure		Type	Doc. type descript.	Item i	NR int. as	No. rng. ext	No. rng.ALE	Updat	Field sel.	Co
▽ ☐ Document types		DB	Dummy purchase order	10	45			SAP	NBF	
▽ ☐ Allowed item categories		ECPO	EBP Standard PO	10	45	44		SAP	NBF	
☐ Link purchase requ		FO	Framework order	10	45	41		SAP	FOF	
		NB	Stan lard PO	10	45	41		SAP	NBF	

Select the Item Category to be allowed and double click on "LINK PURCHASE REQUISITION –DOCUMENT TYPE" on the Dialog Structure.

Enter the combinations that should be allowed for that particular Document Type/Item Category combination.

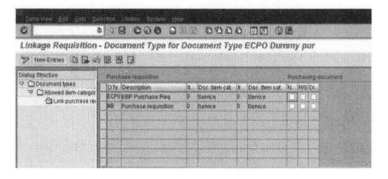

Select 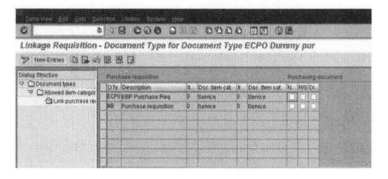 to save the entries.

Repeat this for all relevant Item Categories

Transaction:

IMG Location: IMG > Materials Management > Purchasing >
Purchase Order > Define Document Types

Type	Doc. type descript	Item i	NR int as	No.rng ext	No.rng ALE	Updat	Field sel	Co
DB	Dummy purchase order	10	45	41		SAP	NBF	
ECPO	EBP Standard PO	10	45	44		SAP	NBF	
FO	Framework order	10	45	41		SAP	FOF	
NB	Standard PO	10	45	41		SAP	NBF	
UB	Stock transport ord.	10	45	41		SAP	UBF	T

Select **New Entries**.

Enter the new Document type, Description of the Document Type,
item indicator, internal number range number, external number
range number and field selection key

Type	Doc. type descript	Item i	NR int as	No.rng ext	No.rng ALE	Updat	Field sel.	Co
ECPO	EBP Standard PO	10	45	44		SAP	NBF	

Select the 💾 icon.

To assign the relevant Item Categories, select the document type
created and double click on "ALLOWED ITEM CATEGORIES"
on the Dialog Structure.

Type	Doc. type descript	Item i	NR int as	No.rng ext	No.rng ALE	Updat	Field sel	Co
DB	Dummy purchase order	10	45	41		SAP	NBF	
ECPO	EBP Standard PO	10	45	44		SAP	UBF	
FO	Framework order	10	45	41		SAP	FOF	
NB	Standard PO	10	45	41		SAP	NBF	
UB	Stock transport ord.	10	45	41		SAP	UBF	T

Select the Item Category to be allowed and double click on "LINK PURCHASE REQUISITION –DOCUMENT TYPE" on the Dialog Structure.

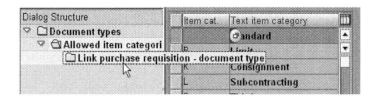

Enter the combinations that should be allowed for that particular Document Type/Item Category combination.

Select  to save the entries.

Repeat this for all relevant Item Categories.

Assign Number Ranges to Vendor Account Groups

Transaction: SPRO

IMG Location: IMG > Financial Accounting > Accounts
Receivable and Accounts Payable > Vendor Accounts > Master
Data > Preparation for Creating Vendor Master Data

Select the Vendor Account Group that you wish to assign the
number Range to.

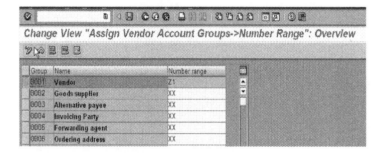

Select the Number Range that you want to assign from the drop-
down menu.

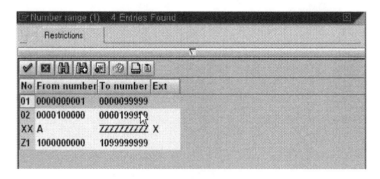

Select the 🖫 to save the assignment.

Define Material Groups

Commodity Codes are identified in SAP as Material Groups. Material Groups are maintained to group together materials that have the same characteristics or are used for similar purposes and enable analyses and search functionality.

A separate Material Group has been set up for the required UNSPSC Commodity Codes. The UNSPSC (United Nations Standard Product and Services Code) is a universally accepted technique of standardizing the classification of goods and services unambiguously. It is a hierarchical classification such that goods and services of similar characteristics can be grouped together to enable communication and cost analyses.

The list that will be used for our purposes are:

26101600	Motors	Motors
30161700	Flooring	Flooring
30171500	Doors	Doors

Maintain Commodity Codes

Transaction: OMSF

Program/Method/Img Location: IMG > Logistics General >
Material Master > Settings for Key Fields > Define Material Groups

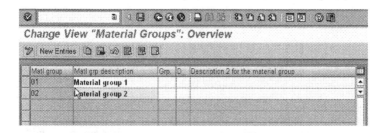

Select **New Entries** to add entries.

Enter the UNSPSC Code and the relecan descriptions.

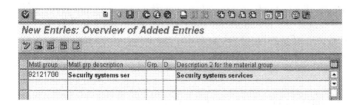

Once you have entered all the UNSPSC codes, select ⊟ to save
your entries.

ALE configuration for IDOC transfer of EBP entered goods receipts and invoices.

The steps in the EBP ALE Setup configuration document must be completed prior to executing the R/3 steps.

The R/3 system needs to have the proper ALE message types maintained and generated in order to accept incoming Goods Receipt postings from the EBP system. The configuration in this document assumes that the ALE model was created in the EBP system and distributed to the R/3 system as a child.

Since the original model view for EBP generated IDoc's was performed in the EBP system, the R/3 system becomes the child to the Parent Model in the EBP system. Therefore, prior to executing the following steps, ensure that the model from the EBP system was distributed properly to the R/3 system. The model should have been transferred through the EBP ALE Setup Configuration steps and should look similar to the following:

Generate Partner Profiles

Transaction: BD64

Menu Path: Environment → Generate partner profiles

Transport: Not Transportable

Once the model has been distributed to the R/3 systems, the partner profiles must likewise be generated in the R/3 system for both R/3 and the EBP logical system ID's.

Click on the model view that was distributed from the EBP system.

Execute the Generate Partner Profiles report from the menu path specified above.

Make sure the Model View field is populated with the EBP view name.

In the Partner System field, enter the logical system ID for the EBP system as well as the R/3 system.

Make sure the "Transfer IDoc Immediately" and "Trigger Immediately" radio buttons are selected.

Model view	to
Partner system	to
Check Run	☐

Default Parameters for Partner Profile

Postprocessing: Authorized processors

Type	US User
ID	Marie Wislocki

Outbound parmtrs.

Version	3 IDoc record types from Version 4.0 onwards
PacketSize	100 IDocs

Output mode
- ◉ Transfer IDoc immediately
- ◯ Collect IDocs and transfer

Inbound parmtrs.

Processing
- ◉ Trigger immediately
- ◯ Trigger by background program

Click on the ⊕ button to generate the profiles.

The output for the report should look similar to the following:

Protocol for generating partner profile

Partner

| System | System ☐ as a partner type already exists |
| System | Partner ☐ as partner has been created |

Port

| System | Port ☐ with RFC destination ☐ has been created |

Outbound params.

| System | Outbound parameters for message type SYNCH SYNCHRON successfully created |

Inbound params.

| System | Input parameter for message type ACC_GOODS_MOVEMENT successfully created |
| | Input parameter for message type MBGMCR successfully created |

Configure Vendor Master

The Vendor Master record is the SAP master record that holds all the information relevant to a particular vendor. Information that is held includes:

Address details

Payment details

Banking details

Purchasing information

The Vendor Master is created within a Plant and Purchasing Organization and the above-mentioned details may be entered applicable to the Plant/Purchasing Organization hierarchy.

Vendor Master Records are also further distinguished by their account group. The account group determines which screens and fields are available and mandatory for this particular vendor to be created.

Making VAT Registration number mandatory (UK)

Transaction: SPRO

Program/Method / Img Location.: IMG > Financial Accounting >
Accounts Payable and Accounts Receivable > Vendor Master>
Master Data > Preparation for creating Vendor Master Data >
Define Account Groups with Screen layout (Vendors)

Select 'Display' button.

Double Click on the 'General Data'.

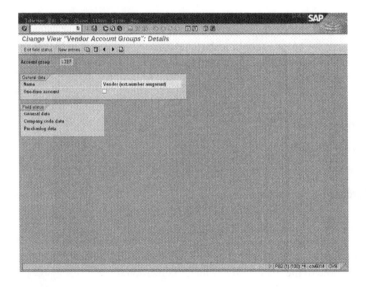

Double click on 'Control'.

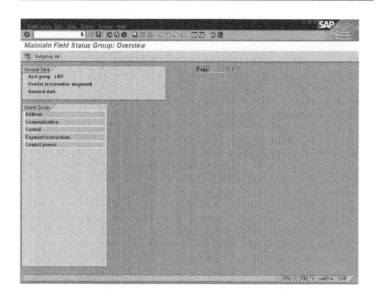

Click on the radio button under the 'Req. Entry' column for VAT registration number.

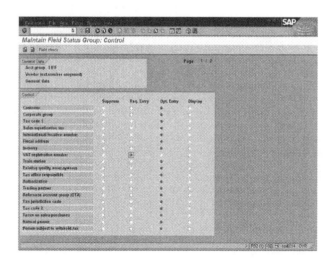

Click on the 'Save' button to save your entry.

JIM STEWART

Section 2: Troubleshooting Guide

Important Programs

Shopping Basket Creation — Program SAPBBPPU99, Service BBPPU99

Account Assignment — Function group BBP_PDH_ACC, Service BBPACCOUNT

Approval work item web transaction — Program SAPMTS1 0008069H, Service TS_TS10008069H

Shopping Basket Status — Program SAPBBPPU02, Service BBPPU02

Login and launch pad — Program SAPBBPST01, Service BBPSTART

Shared MIME / JavaScript / HTML Business / Java Applet files — service BBPGLOBAL

Confirmations (Goods Receipt) — Function group BBP_CF, Service BBPCF02

Little known configuration options

Many of the activities that you will perform in the EBP system are not accessible via menus, and the configuration areas are not available from the IMG.

Adding a new attribute to the organizational plan

Use transaction SM30 to add entries to table T770MATTR.

The attribute must first be created in the attributes section. This includes linking the attribute with a data dictionary type definition, and determining whether multiple values are permissible or whether local values should override inherited values. Customer specific attributes must start with Z.

Once the attribute has been created, include the attribute in the EBP scenario, and assign the 0 (organizational unit) and S (position) object types to the attribute to allow it to be assigned to org units/positions on the organizational plan.

The attributes can then be accessed via transaction PPOMA_CRM in the same way as standard SAP attributes.

Opening extra fields in the account assignment screens

Use transaction SM30 to add entries to table BBP_C_ACCF.

This table determines which fields are open for display/change in the extended account assignment screens. For each account category, only one field must be marked as the main field. More fields can be added as secondary fields to be opened. To find the field names, examine the field list of screen 2000 of function group BBP_PDH_ACC.

Working with Workflow

Shopping Cart Approval Workflows

The most frequently changed workflows are the shopping basket approval workflows.

Several approval workflows are provided as examples. These are working examples that can be used as-is if desired. Many customers do use them as-is, particularly for pilots. The main workflows are:

WS 10000060— No approval (i.e. automatic approval)

WS 10000129 — One step approval (approval by manager, i.e. chief position in same org unit).

WS 10000031 — Two step approval (first approval is by manager, second approval is by manager's manager)

WS 10000276 — Spending limit approval (approval is by nominated approval manager for the relevant approval limit, based on the total value of the shopping cart)

* WS1000133 – n-step approval with BADI

All use the sub workflow WS 10000245 which contains the after approval processing.

NOTE: If customer-specific workflows are created they should also use sub workflow

WS 100000245 for after approval processing.

Additionally, a shopping basket approval wizard is accessible from the IMG in the workflow section under the Enterprise Buyer section (or Business-to-Business Procurement section in earlier releases). The wizard enables new workflows to be created, e.g. if a 3 step approval workflow is needed.

There are also workflows for confirmations (goods receipts) and invoices.

Copying Workflows

Use transaction PFTC_COP to copy workflows.

To change the copied workflows use transaction PFTCCHG.

Changing Workflows

Use transaction PFTCCHG to change workflows.

You should only change your own copies — never change the standard workflows.

When changing any shopping cart approval workflow, be careful how you affect the applet for the approval display in the "Check Status" (BBPPUO2) web transaction. Any steps you add that should NOT appear in the display should have the flag "step not in workflow log" turned on in the workflow step. This flag removes the step from the graphical workflow log, which is the source of the data for the approval display. The step can still be seen in the technical view of the log so that a workflow administrator can resolve any problems.

Start Conditions

Start conditions are accessible from the IMG. Transaction SWBPROCTJREMENT.

The start condition editor enables:

a) Activation/deactivation of triggering event linkage to workflows

b) Creation/change/deletion of logical expression to act as start condition

The check function module SWB CHECK PB START COND EVAL evaluates the start condition. Therefore start conditions are only relevant if the check function module has been included in the event type linkage (accessed via transaction SWETYPV) of the triggering event/workflow in question (this situation may change in later releases — it's likely that checking of start conditions will be automatic for all workflows).

The logical expression can be based on:

Constants — e.g. $500

Workflow system elements — e.g. workflow initiator

Object attributes — e.g. "requisitioner" of shopping basket

Customer-specific object attributes can be used.

The key point to remember in creating the logical expression is that only values known at event creation time can be used. For instance, approver could NOT be used as this is not known until after the workflow has started.

Creating new object attributes

Create a subtype of the standard SAP business object type (transaction SW01).

The subtype must start with Z, and the subtype program must start with Z.

Change status of subtype to "implemented" and then to "released".

Generate the subtype.

Use system-wide delegation to delegate the SAP business object type to the new subtype.

Create new attributes on the subtype.

Implement the matching code in the subtype program as necessary and regenerate.

When creating new attributes for a subtype of BUS2 121 (Requirement Coverage Request, alias the shopping cart), be careful that you cater for both an existing shopping cart and a temporary shopping cart. If you don't cater for the temporary shopping cart and you use these attributes in start conditions or agent determination the approval preview will fail or fail to show the correct approvers. To understand how to access the temporary shopping cart make sure you look at the programming underneath the standard BUS2 121 program (mostly this is done by using IMPORT FROM MEMORY to read the temporary structures output by the shopping cart program SAPBBPPU99).

Options for creating new role resolutions

The full SAP Business Workflow environment is available. This gives the following options for new role resolutions:

• Standard role based on "responsibilities" created via transaction PFAC. This allows input criteria to be specified as role container elements. Possible input criteria combinations (which may include ranges and/or lists of single values) are then defined as responsibility areas and agents assigned to the responsibility areas. It is also possible to assign "priorities" to the responsibility criteria combinations. This allows certain criteria to be assessed prior to others, e.g. look for a specific match, if not found, assess more general entries. Criteria with higher priorities are assessed before lower priorities, highest priority is 99, and lowest priority is 1.

NOTE: Essentially this is equivalent to creating a customer table of criteria combinations mapped against agents, which could then be evaluated by a customer specific role function module. However responsibility roles do not require further programming, so it is recommended that they be used in place of customer tables.

Standard role based on a customer specific role function module created via transaction PFAC. This may be useful in complex situations. For instance, the place where agents need to be determined based on information in the backend R/3 system. One example, determining the cost centre manager from fields in the cost centre master data in the backend R3 system. Any agents determined must be mapped to valid EBP organizational units/positions or to valid EBP userids.

There are other mechanisms available (e.g. SAP organizational object assignment or SAP office distribution lists) however the above two methods are the most useful within the context of EBP.

Including new role resolutions in Ad hoc agent assignment

Ad hoc agent assignment has two major purposes within EBP.

1. It allows the default approvers to be calculated at the commencement of the workflow so that current and future approvers can be displayed as part of shopping basket status and the approval workitem.

2. Through coding in the shopping basket status and approval workitem programs, the change approver function can be used to change the selected agent dynamically.

To include role resolutions in ad hoc agent assignment, the following steps are needed.

1. Create a subtype of standard SAP business object type AAGENT to represent the new role.

2. Use code in standard object type ASBMANAGER as a template for code in new subtype.

3. Redefine and change the code in the "Create" method of the new subtype to determine the default approver as needed. This involves firstly determining the input criteria, e.g. by evaluating attributes of object references in the approval workflow container, then evaluating the new role resolution. If a responsibility role was created, function module RH can be called to evaluate the role. Otherwise, the role function module itself is called at this point. The list of agents must be resolved down to user names for EBP. Function module RH_STRUC_GET can be used to do this (see coding example in function module SWX_GET_MANAGER).

4. In the "Create" method, don't forget to check whether the shopping cart is temporary or existing. If temporary, you will need to send the list of agents to a container element called "Agents",

otherwise the agent list will not display on the approval preview. The program code underneath the "Create" method for the standard business object ASBMANAGER shows how to do this.

5. Create the new workflow either via shopping basket approval wizard or as a copy of one of the existing approval workflows. In the workflow container, set up an approver container element referencing the new subtype. In the approval step, assign the "Agents" attribute of the approver container element as the responsible agent.

At runtime, an initial step (or basic data of the workflow definition in later releases) of the workflow runs the "Execute" method of the "Ad hoc factory" object. This step instantiates all workflow container elements that reference object type AAGENT or any of its subtypes, and executes the relevant "Create" method to determine the default approver. That is, at this point the default approvers are calculated so that they can be shown in the shopping basket status display, and in all approval workitems.

The default approver determined in the "Create" method becomes the selected agent of the approval step, providing of course that they are also possible agents of the approval task.

Possible agents of the approval workflow have the authority to change the approver either via the shopping basket status (for the requisitioner), or via the approval workitem (for reviewers/approvers — e.g. to change subsequent approvers). The code to change the agent has been directly coded into the programs behind shopping basket status and the web transaction for the approval workitem.

The change approver function allows the user to change the selected agent of the approval workitem to another possible agent. Therefore, the change approver function is only relevant when the approval task has been assigned to specific possible agents (e.g. via security roles [activity groups]) and NOT to general task.

Note that forwarding the workitem to another possible agent has the same effect as changing the approver at the current approval level — so workflow administrators can redirect these workitems via SAPGUI and do not need to go out to the web to do this.

Workitems via the web

All standard tasks to be performed via the web have:

- Object type FORM and method HTMLPROCESS

- A link to a generated web transaction (via menu path GOTO →
Web Transaction) program

- ITS service/template files matching the web transaction program

The generated web transaction program consists of four (4) main
screens:

- Screen 50— Entry screen for pickup of the workitem id

- Screen 100 — Main screen for execution of the workitem

- Screen 150— Main screen for start of a workflow (NOT USED IN
EBP)

- Screen 200 — Confirmation messages screen

In addition some web transactions have been significantly changed
from the original generated web transaction. For example, the web
transaction for the shopping basket approval uses screen 100 as a
main screen to call a number of sub screens to display all the
approval information from the approval workitem.

Note that several standard tasks may be connected to the same web
transaction. For instance, a number of separate but similar standard
tasks link to the web transaction for shopping basket approval. This
enables different possible agent assignment per standard task, but
consistency of the approval workitem operation.

Email notification of outstanding approvals

In EBP, program RSWUWFMLEC is used to create email notifications of outstanding workitems. This program is a variant of the standard R3 email notification program

RSWUWFML.

The following pre-conditions must be met before email notifications can be sent:

a) EBP system must be configured to be able to send email to an Internet email address via the appropriate mail server. That is, SAP Connect or SMTP or similar must be installed between EBP and the mail server.

b) An email address must be assigned to the workflow system user (i.e. user id WF-BATCH) as the sender address. This email address must be acceptable to the mail server, i.e. not produce an error when it is used as the sender address. Transaction SWU3 is used to assign the email address to the workflow system user id WF-BATCH.

c) The user(s) to whom the email notification is to be sent have the organizational plan attribute FORWARD_WI (Flag: Forward Work Item) set to "X" and have a valid email address assigned to their EBP user id. These can be checked via the standard EBP web transactions "Change Attributes" and "Change settings" respectively.

d) For EBP 2MB systems ensure OSS notes 354082 and 353746 have been applied (included in patch SAPKU2OBO8).

Program RSWUWFMLEC should be scheduled to run on a regular basis, e.g. once every 15 minutes. A user with appropriate authority must be assigned to the job. By preference this should be a generic batch ("System") user id with SAP ALL authority.

Assign the user id WF-BA TCH as the executor of the RS WUWFMLEC step.

Ensure the user id assigned to the job has an email address in their user master (otherwise you will get a transmission failure error, because the sender does not have an email address).

The parameter "One mail per work item" should be turned on to ensure the email contains details of the specific work item including a hyperlink to the workitem. The web server/port used in the hyperlink are taken from the organizational plan attribute ITS DEST (Current ITS of user).

The parameter "Protocol: Everything" should be turned on so that the number of mails sent successfully/unsuccessfully is written to the spool list (this is useful in tracking down problems).

Emails are only sent if there are outstanding workitem that have been created as of the last run date/time of the job. If the user touches the workitem prior to job execution, no mail will be sent.

Note that emails are never automatically deleted. It is up to the user to delete the email once it is no longer required.

Debugging of the email notification:

a) Check the user's organizational attributes using function module BBP GET ATTRIBUTES in test mode.

b) Use transactions SWU3 and/or SUO 1 to check that an email address has been assigned to the workflow system user id WF-BATCH.

c) Check that the RSWUWFMLEC job is running. Check any spool lists from the job. If there are no spool lists, no outstanding workitems were found. If the spool list indicates, "Transmission failed", most likely cause is a bad email address for user id WF-BATCH.

d) Use transaction SCOT to check that emails have been sent to the mail server correctly. The "Internal Trace" utility is useful to debug problems in sending the mail to the mail server. Emails in "Waiting" status can be pushed through to the mail server manually with the "Start send process" function. Emails in "In Transit" status have been sent to the mail server. Emails in "Error" status indicate a problem at the mail server.

e) Use transaction SOST to view each message sent and specific problems per message. This transaction also shows whether the message has been created but not yet sent to the mail server.

f) If there is a problem at the mail server, contact the mail server owner for assistance with tracing the email through the mail server.

g) If necessary, change the parameters "From work item creation date" and "From work item creation time" to recreate mails for outstanding workitems that have been previously processed by the RSWUWFMLEC program.

Meta-BAPIs

This chapter will help you understand meta-BAPI behavior.

Each meta-BAPI is a function module beginning with META_*

Whenever a backend system call is involved, meta-BAPIs are used to determine and call the appropriate function module for the type of backend system.

Meta-BAPIs are specific to a particular function, e.g. "Validate account assignment", "Create purchase order". These functions are also expressed as methods of objects, e.g. Purchase order object BUS2012, method "CreateFromData".

The meta-BAPI determines the type of the backend system (e.g. local, R3 version 3.1, R3 version 4.OB, R/3 version 4.5B, R/3 version 4.6A, non-R/3 system), and then reads the matching entry on table BBP_FUNCTION_MAP for the relevant object/method/backend type combination to find the backend specific function module to be called.

The backend specific function module exists in the EBP system. Its' purpose is to prepare and reformat data then call the relevant routine(s) for that backend type. All backend specific function modules for the same object /method have the same parameters, i.e. the meta-BAPI makes one dynamic function call and assumes that parameters are the same for all the function modules.

Calling customer-specific function modules from meta-BAPIs If desired, e.g. to pass additional information to a BAPI extension, customers can create their own backend specific function modules. The same parameters as other backend specific function modules for the same object/method must be used. Within the function module, additional code can be added to extract additional data or massage existing data prior to send to the backend, and/or to call additional or replacement function modules in the relevant backend system.

The customer-specific function module must be added to table BBP_FUNCTION_MAP in place of the standard SAP function module for that object/method/backend type.

Popular Modifications / Enhancements

This chapter includes some of the most common development requests and quick solutions.

• Use of the catalog content BADI to reformat and/or map supplier specific values (such as product categories) to desired values.

• Use of the catalog content BAI to reformat and/or map special fields in the. OCI (e.g. customer fields) to appropriate table/fields for further processing.

• Modifications to the shopping basket creation transaction and associated services/templates to hide fields (e.g. to hide free text entry area), or to make new fields/screens available. For example, tracking number.

• Modifications to the shopping basket creation transaction and associated services/templates to change suggested defaults, e.g. default unit of measure, default catalogue

• Modifications to the account assignment function group and associated services/templates to make new fields available. E.g. activity type.

• Modifications to the shopping basket status transaction and associated service/templates changed to hide fields or to make new fields/screens available.

• Use of the backend object determination BADI to reassign shopping basket items to desired backend object determination.

• Use of backend object creation BADIs to prepare additional information for passing to the backend object, e.g. tracking number.

• Modifications to the web transaction for shopping basket approval and associated service/templates to display additional information as part of the approval workitem.

• Search helps using backend data, e.g. in the account assignment screen, permit a search on internal orders when the "order" account assignment category has been chosen.

Business Add-Ins (BADIs)

Purpose of BADIs

Business Add-Ins are essentially a new form of user-exit. The BADI approach provides greater flexibility than the user-exit approach.

For instance, it is possible for several separate implementations of the BADI to exist in parallel (although only one implementation may be active at any one time). This is very useful when comparing the effect of using different source code within the

BADI.

It is also possible to define multiple implementations of the BADI and use a filter to determine which implementation is executed at runtime depending on the runtime data involved.

Implementing BADIs

BADI implementations can be accessed via the IMG or via transaction SE 18.

Use se19 to make modifications to your custom class implementation.

Each BADI has a definition name, e.g.
BBP_CATALOG_TRANSFER. The essential part of the BADI is
the interface and the associated method.

"Implementing" a BADI involves creating a class and associated
method based on the interface and method specified in the BADI.

Implementation commences by pressing the execute icon in the
IMG, or use menu path Implementation> Create in SE 18. As part
of implementation a new class based on the interface is
automatically generated. You must provide a Z name for the new
class.

On the "Interface" tab of the implementing class, you can see the
interface, the implementing class and the method name.

Once the new class has been created you can then enter your source
code in the method (double-click on the method name to enter the
source code area). The source code of a BADI can include calls to
function modules, select statements to database tables, code
manipulating data, etc.

However to work with the method you must know the parameters of
the method. To do this you need to look at the interface or
implementing class (double-click on either from the "Interface" tab
of the implementing class or BADI definition). In the interface or
implementing class display, the available methods are listed, cursor
position on the matching method name for your BADI and press the
"Parameters" button to see the parameters and their reference types.

Note that as BADIs are coded using object-oriented principles ALL
parameter tables are tables WITHOUT header line.

That is, to read them in the method you need to use explicit
workareas. For example,

```
Data: catalog_wa like line of
catalog_content.

Loop at catalog_content into catalog_wa.

Move catalog wa—description to

Endloop.
```

Activating/Deactivating BADIs

Once the code has been entered, syntax checked and generated, the BADI must be activated. This happens in two places. First, while in the source code, the source code must be activated. Second, while in the implementing class, the implementing class must be activated.

Both source code and implementing class must be active before the system will use the BADI.

To deactivate a BADI, deactivate the implementing class is sufficient. There's no need to deactivate the source code.

BADI Limitations

The parameters of the BADI cannot be changed, i.e. you cannot add or remove parameters. Only the contents of the parameters can be changed.

The BADI is called from a program. It is not possible to change the point at which the BADI is called. It is not possible to access global data of the calling program.

To determine where the BADI is called, i.e. which is its' calling program, the implementing class display includes a "where-used list" button.

One popular, but ill-advised solution is to simply "break out" from the encapsulation of the BADI call to a customer function module. Simply create a function module that imports the needed objects and exports them back. In the context of a function module call, you can have access to any SAP or table data that you need without the restrictions of ABAP objects.

BAPI Extensions

Purpose of BAPI Extensions

BAPI Extensions allow additional information (e.g. customer specific) to be passed from the EBP system to the backend R3 system, e.g. when creating purchase requisitions or purchase orders. BAPI extensions are available in certain backend R/3 system releases (OSS notes for the particular BAPI must be checked to determine which releases/minimum hotpacks provide extensions to the desired BAPI).

The real benefit of this technique is that it allows additional data to be passed into the BAPI. This caters not only for customer fields, e.g. customer-specific fields in account assignment, but also existing standard SAP fields that are not included in the standard data for the BAPI.

In conjunction with BADIs and/or customer specific meta-BAPIs in the EBP system, BAPI extensions applied in the backend R3 system allow more data to be passed than is included in standard EBP.

For example, when passing customer specific account assignment data from EBP to the backend R3 system.

Using BAPI Extensions — BAPIPO_CREATE Example This describes the basic operation of extensions using BAPI_PO_CREATE (purchase order creation) as an example.

---

1. You must have applied the patch that includes the BAPI extensions for the desired BAPI. Descriptions of the extensions for the BAPI are usually found in OSS notes. For instance, OSS note 336589 for purchase orders, 336692 for purchase requisitions. Check the notes carefully as the patches are specific and may only apply to certain R/3 releases.

2. The BAPI will include an EXTENSIONIN table parameter with structure BAPIPAREX. This parameter is used to pass the additional information into the target system (i.e. the system owning the BAPI). Note: There is an equivalent parameter for passing additional details to the source system, EXTENSIONOUT. You need to look at the specific BAPI and relevant OSS notes to determine whether this parameter exists for the desired BAPI.

3. The first 30 characters (field STRUCTURE) of the EXTENSIONIN parameter is filled with the name of the structure used to define the format of the additional details, e.g. BAPI_TE_PO_ITEMS. After the structure name, the remaining fields are filled with the additional data in the matching format. A maximum of 960 bytes of data may be passed per EXTENSIONIN row not including the structure name. The 960 bytes of data are split across 4 fields of 240 bytes each— VALUEPARTI to VALUEPART4. You may add as many rows as necessary to the EXTENSIONIN table.

The structures used to define the format are known formats to the BAPI. For instance, BAPI_PO_CREATE allows structures BAPI_TE_PO_HEADER, BAPIJE_P0_ITEMS, and BAPI_TE_PO_ITEM_ACCOUNT to be used to pass additional header, item and account assignment details respectively.

5. Within the known structures, key information is held to match the additional data to the standard data. For instance, BAPI_TE_PO_ITEMS contains the purchase order item number to be matched to the standard item data passed to the BAPI in the table parameter P0_ITEMS.

6. After the key information, the required additional data is added. This may be done via a CI include if available, or via append structures. However it is vital that all fields included in the additional data must match be created with field names matching

the target structures. The OSS note specific to the desired BAPI's extension will identify the target structure. For instance, the target structure for purchase order items is EKPO. So the additional data fields in BAPIJEPOJTEMS must have the same field names as their target fields in structure EKPO. Note: This may mean ignoring the usual naming convention of ZZ* for fields in append structures.

7. At runtime, after the standard data has been used to fill the target structures, the additional data in the EXTENSIONIN parameter is also used to fill the target structures. Note: This is usually done via a MOVE- CORRESPONDING — so there is no opportunity to manipulate the additional data at this point. However f the BAPI also contains user exits, they may allow some manipulation of the additional data prior to the MOVE-CORRESPONDING command.

Further Information

More information on this and related BAPI enhancement/extension techniques is found in SAPNET alias BAPI, in the "Developer's Guide" section for BAPIs.

Modification Assistant

Process for applying modifications

You still require an object key from OSS. As in previous releases, this is usually requested when you first enter the program/screen/etc. in change mode.

In change mode, code/screen remains protected but new pushbuttons appear:

Insert — adding a block of code, adding screen elements (e.g. new fields) Replace — comments out existing code, gives a copy of existing code to modify Delete — comments out existing code — be careful that integrity of program is maintained, i.e. that it can still be successfully syntax checked and generated Remove modification — returns the program, etc. to SAP standard. Also removes the relevant link on the modification log.

The blocks are marked with:

- An opening comment line starting with *#{

- A closing comment line *#}

- When each new modification is made, once a change request is assigned to the object, the change request number is automatically included in the opening comment line.

How do I find existing modifications?

The modification log (transaction SE95) gives a breakdown and in many cases, double-click access to modified objects. This is an excellent resource as an overall view of all the modifications in the system. It includes all modified objects even "safe" modifications such as append structures.

Upgrade Issues

Transaction SPDD and SPAU are still used to adjust the objects. However changes made via the modification assistant are analyzed at a fine granularity, e.g. the subroutine level. Automatic reapplication of modifications is available where SAP standard has not changed. Semi automatic reapplication of modifications is available where SAP standard has changed but it is still easily determined by the system where the modification belongs. In more complex situations, a split screen editor supports manual reapplication of modifications. The split screen editor allows identification, for example, of each individual modification block and the ability to opt to remove/copy to a nominated position/manually adjust code. The manual reapplication of modifications can be entered multiple times, and requires positive confirmation that all modifications in that object have been completed.

Limitations of modification assistant

Modification assistant is NOT used for ITS files such as services and templates. This means particular care must be taken to record all changes made to services and templates.

Modification assistant is NOT used for changes to messages classes and messages. Modification assistant is NOT used for changes to business object type programs.

Upgrade from 2.0 to 4.0 goes surprisingly smooth, with the exception of vendors. See section on debugging vendors for more specific information.

Working with ITS services/templates

A separate virtual ITS/web server is created for EBP as part of installation. Ensure that an Admin ITS is also created on the same machine for remote administration of the EBP ITS. Multiple ITS/web servers may exist on the same machine, e.g. DEV EBP and TST EBP, if desired. Each ITS is given either a separate port number or a separate I.P. number. Sufficient memory needs to exist for all ITS to run concurrently (128MB per virtual ITS + 32MB for the Admin ITS).

It is ESSENTIAL that all team members know the start URL for EBP. This is always the URL to the BBPSTART service.

That is,

http://<EBPwebserver>:<EBPport>/scripts/wgate/bbpstart/?

Basis team members also need to know the URL, userid and password for the admin service.

http://<ADMwebserver>:<ADMport>/scripts/wgate/admin!

The default user id is ITSADMIN, and the default password is INIT.

Ensure the JACOR NT service has been configured and started for each virtual ITS/web server involved. This enables publishing of service/template files from the EBP system to the ITS/web server.

Publishing of ITS service/template files from the EBP system occurs due to:

a) Patches / hot packs being applied — usually by running report

W3_PUBLISH_SER VICES

b) Modifications/enhancements of existing templates and development of new templates via transaction SE8O

PLEASE NOTE: There is no need to install or use SAP@WebStudio to work with the ITS. Transaction SE8O provides all essential utilities for creating, changing, publishing and transporting ITS service/template files. The only exceptions are the GLOBAL service (which is maintained via the Admin ITS).

The SAP@WebStudio product, however, can be used to efficiently make changes to templates, and it can also be used to debug and update templates in conjunction with a professional HTML editing tool such as Dreamweaver.

Most Important Services

Service GLOBAL holds the reference to the EBP system and the exit URL. Unless a specific exit URL is desired, default value of— should be the entry point, i.e. http://<EBPwebserver>:<EBPport>/scripts/wgate/bbpstart/!?—language=en

Service BBPGLOBAL holds all the shared MIME files, including shared HTMLBusiness function files, Javascript files and Java applet files.

Service BBPPU99 is the main shopping basket creation service.

Service BBPACCOUNT controls the account assignment display for a number of other services such as shopping basket creation, confirmation, invoices, etc.

Service BBPPUO2 is the shopping basket status service.

Service BBPCFO2 is the confirmation (i.e. goods receipt/service entry sheet) service.

Services starting with TS_TS* are services related to workflow workitems.

Standard system templates, scripts, HTMLBusiness function files, etc. are included in the templates directory under the "SYSTEM" service folder. This includes the workplace integration (WP1NTEGRATION), and search help (SEARCHHELP) files. All runtime ITS error message templates are also in the system folder.

Modifying ITS service template files

Modification assistant is NOT available for ITS service/template files. Version management is available for ITS service/template files but lacks certain functionality (temporary versions are ok, but patches tend to not to preserve the versioning). Therefore it is ESSENTIAL that changes to ITS service/template files are adequately recorded. Always make a backup copy of the file, ideally creating a separate file directory for the backup files.

To access the service/template files, from transaction SE8O, choose the object type "Internet Service" and enter/search for the appropriate Internet service name. Double- clicking on the service name itself accesses the service file. In the launch pad, expand the service to access the theme, expand the theme to access the templates. Double- clicking on the theme itself accesses the language resource file (if existing). Double- clicking on the template name accesses the template. When working with template files it is worthwhile using the "hide launchpad" button, as many of the files are greater than 80 characters across.

Multimedia files within a service are also accessible via transaction SE80 in the same way. However not all multimedia files can be viewed or modified via SE8O. Import/export of multimedia files is more likely.

Publishing ITS files

In transaction SE8O, choose menu options Utilities → Settings. Go to the ITS tab. Select the specific ITS from the drop-down list. If no ITS appear or the desired ITS does not appear this indicates that the IACOR NT service has not been configured and should be resolved with whichever Basis person is responsible for the ITS installation.

It is also possible to publish the files to a local file directory (e.g. for backup, for documentation purposes) by selecting that option and entering an appropriate directory.

NOTE: Publishing settings last for the duration of the logon session only.

To publish the files, display the relevant service in the launchpad, right-click on either the service or the particular file to access the "Publish" option on the context menu. When multiple files are to be published for the same service, right-click on the service and select "Publish..." → "Complete Service".

After publishing, the message "Object published successfully" should appear in the message line. Any problems/warnings should result in a dialog box appearing with a log list of objects attempted to be published and appropriate red/yellow/green icons indicating error/warning/success messages.

If the message "Application log could not be displayed" appears, this indicates that there is insufficient authority to show the log. This will only appear if there was an error/warning with the publishing. As warnings appear when new service/theme directories are created on the ITS, it is worthwhile publishing again in this case as a second publish should then return, "Object published successfully".

Special files to modify

Runtime ITS error messages need to be personalized for the company involved. Do this by changing the HEAD.html and TAIL.html templates in the "PM" productive mode) directory within the "SYSTEM" folder in the templates directory. Ensure the company's logo is included in HEAD.html template. Ensure references to the company's help desk are included in the TAIL.html template. Remove references to SAP AG and SAP logos in both templates.

Add the company logos to the start and home pages by replacing the following multimedia files within the BBPGLOBAL service, theme 99:

1. Company logo — LOGO.GIF in the IMAGES/START directory.

2. Main home page picture — BG START.jpg in the IMAGES/HOMEPAGE directory

3. Default photo picture (which user's can personalize) — DEFAULT_PHOTO.gif in the PHOTO directory.

Assessing Graphic dimensions

So that suitable logos/home page graphics can be chosen or created, it's useful to be able to assess the dimensions of these graphics.

The simplest way to do this is to open the graphic on it's own in the web browser screen, e.g. by URL http://<webserver>:<port>/sap/its/mimes/bbpglobal/99/images/start/logo.gif

Right-click on the graphic and go to "Properties" to find the dimensions in pixels. Remember that only pixels matter on web pages, as pixels are a measure relative to the screen resolution.

If an existing customer-specific graphic of different dimensions is to be used in place of the default graphics, it may be necessary to use a graphics program, e.g. Microsoft PhotoDraw, to adjust the dimensions of the customer-specific graphic so that it fits the EBP web page.

Adding search helps

Create a search-help in the usual way from the data dictionary (transaction SE11).

One possible difference with EBP is that the data to be selected may exist only in the backend system. To use data in the backend system, create the search-help without a selection method. Instead enter a search-help exit.

Attach the search-help to the relevant screen field via the screen field attributes, or to the data element of the relevant screen field.

Using a search-help exit to read backend data

Search-help exits are function modules. Create the function module by copying function module F4IF_SFILP_EXIT_EXAMPLE.

Add the search help type pool to the global data of the function group and any other data definitions needed to support the search help exit code.

Example:

```
Type-pools: SHLP.

Data:  backend system like rfcdes—rfcdest, Backend
destination washlpselopt like ddshselopt,
        "Selection options
```

```
order type type bapi2075 2—order type,  "Selection
criteria order_list type standard table of
bap120751. "Output list
```

To retrieve data from the backend R3 system, replace the section "STEP SELECT" with suitable code.

Example Code:

```
If calicontrol-step = 'SELECT'.

*Determine the backend logical system, e.g. by
reading table BBPBACKENDDEST

*Read the search criteria — example below uses a
parameter ORDER_TYPE

* created in the searchhelp

Loop at ship—selopt into washipselopt.

Case washlpselopt-shlpfield.

When 'ORDER TYPE'

If wa shlp selopt—sign = 'I'

And wa ship selopt-option = 'EQ

Order_type = washipselopt-low.

Endif.

Endcase.

Endloop.

*Retrieve the data from the backend R/3 system,
e.g. via a suitable

BAP I

Call function 'BAPIINTERNALORDERGETLIST'

Destination backend system

Exporting

Order_type   = order_type

Tables
```

```
Order_list    = order_list.

If sy—subrc ne 0.

Callcontrol—step = 'EXIT'.

Exit.

Endif.

*Format the data for the searchhelp Call function
'F4UT RESULTS MAP' Tables

Shlp Tab      = ship_tab

Record_Tab    = record_tab

Source_Tab    = order_list

Changing

Ship   = shlp

Cailcontrol = cailcontrol

Exceptions

If sy—subrc = 0.

Cailcontrol—step = 'DISP'.

Else.

Calicontrol—step = 'EXIT'.

Endif.

Exit.

Endif.
```

Adjusting HTML templates

Add the help button immediately after the relevant field on the HTML template of the relevant service.

Example:

```
'F4HelpButton(bbpforrnname, "S_SCREEN_ACCDET-
ORDER_NO", "Find Internal Order, "Go")'
```

Parameter 1 — form name

Parameter 2 technical screen field name

Parameter 3 Search title text

Parameter 4 Go text

Add SEARCHHELP.html to the relevant main service/theme (e.g. if adding help to account assignment service BBPACCOUNT, you need to identify the main service such as BBPPU99). The new SEARCHHELP.html should be copied from an existing service, e.g. BBPMAININT. SEARCHHELP.html contains generic code suitable for displaying all search helps so there is no need to change this template.

Add texts for SEARCH_SHELP (e.g. "Go") and CANCEL_SHELP (e.g. "Cancel") to the language resource file for the main service/theme.

Customer-Specific Account Assignment

This section uses an example of a customer specific field "ZZEXTRAFLD" that exists in the coding block (i.e. structure CI_COBL) in the backend system. In this example, ZZEXTRAFLD needs to be added to the account assignment screen of the shopping basket item so that the user can enter a value into it. The value is then validated and eventually passed to the requisition(s) and/or purchase order(s) created in the backend.

It's worthwhile implementing the passing of the field first and testing that it is passed to the backend correctly before implementing validation.

Usually the field is also required for valid confirmations to be created. Further changes are necessary to pick up the field from the purchase order and pass it to the goods receipt or service entry sheet being created.

Tip: Ensure you have a new development class, as append structures must be saved to a development class; they cannot be made "local objects".

To add ZZEXTRAFLD to the Shopping Basket Account Assignment

Screen

Use an append structure to add field ZZEXTRAFLD to table BBP_PDS_ACCDAT.

This will allow access to the text description of ZZEXTRAFLD.

Use an append structure to add field ZZEXTRAFLD to table BBP_OCI_ENRACCT. This is the account assignment table for the shopping basket. This will allow access to the input/output (I/O) properties of ZZEXTRAFLD.

Use an append structure to add field ZZEXTRAFLD to table REQACCT. This is used to store the user-entered ZZEXTRAFLD value on the account assignment table for the shopping basket.

In Function group BBP_PDH_ACC, the field may be added to screen 1000, screen 2000 or both. As a general rule, add to screen 1000 if the new field is mandatory for all shopping basket items; add to screen 2000 if the new field is optional.

• Screen 1000— Add ZZEXTRAFLD to the screen as an I/O field (get from program T_SCREENACCLIST-ZZEXTRAFLD) and text field (get from dictionary BBP_PDACC-ZZEXTRAFLD) added to screen with modification group 2 set to EDI.

• Screen 1000 — Include the new field in the "... on-chain request" statement in the PAI section of the flow logic.

• Screen 2000 — Add ZZEXTRAFLD to the screen as an 1I0 field (get from program S_SCREEN_ACCDET-ZZEXTRAFLD) and text field (get from dictionary BBP_PDACC-ZZEXTRAFLD) added to screen with modification group 2 set to EDI and modification group 3 set to 002.

Which fields are available for different account assignment categories is controlled via table BBP_C_ACCF. Via transaction SE16 (BBP 2.0B) or SM30 (EBP 2.0), in table BBP_C_ACCF, add new entry for the appropriate account assignment category and account field ZZEXTRAFLD, main account flag is off

Via transaction SE8O, to Internet Service BBPACCOUNT, theme 99, add code to templates `SAPLBBPPDHACC1 000_PU99, SAPLBBPPDHACC1 000_PU99, SAPLBBP_PDH_ACC_2000_PU99`, and `SAPLBBP_PDH_ACC_2000_PU02` to

include ZZEXTRAFLD. Make sure you adjust the field titles as well as including your I/O field.

To Pass ZZEXTRAFLD from Shopping Basket to Purchase

Requisition/Order

In the backend system:

The BAPI parameter EXTENSION1N will be used to pass the additional account

Assignment data.

Refer to the BAPI Extensions section on how to set up the field in the relevant BAPI extension structures e.g. BAPI for purchase requisitions, BAPI_TE_PO_ITEM_ACCOUNT for purchase orders.

In the EBP system:

Ensure the copies of the relevant BAPI extension structures exist in EBP. If any are missing, it may be necessary to create a "Z*" copy of them in the EBP system.

Ensure the structure definitions match exactly between EBP and the backend.

Use the modification assistant to change B45A_REQUISITION_CREATE and/or B45A_PO_CREATE as necessary to:

a) Read table REQREF to find the matching shopping basket for the purchase order or requisition. Note: item number is empty on REQREF at this point.

b) Read the matching ZZEXTRAFLD value from table REQACCT

c) Fill the relevant BAPI extension structure, e.g.

`BAPI_TE_PO_ITEM_ACCOUNT` for purchase orders.

d) Fill the EXTENSION1N parameter table

e) Call the relevant BAPI, e.g. BAPI_PO_CREATE (for purchase orders) using the EXTENSIONIN parameter table

To validate ZZEXTRAFLD during Shopping Basket Creation

Note that when account assignment is validated, any program-based validation rules

including active customer user-exits (such as EXIT_SAPLKACB_002) are checked.

However screen-based rules, e.g. field is mandatory are NOT checked.

Checking of customer fields:

In backend, change `BBP4X_COD1NGBLOCK_CHECK` to

a) Optionally import `BBPCOBL_CUST` as a table of `BAPICOBL_CI`.

b) Add "`DATA: CHECK_CUSTOMERFIELDS LIKE BAPICOBL_CUST.`

c) In the loop of table `BBPCOBL`, map data to `CHECK_CODINGBLOCK` (for the call to `BAPI_ACCSERV_CHECKACCASSIGNMT`), by reading the matching `BBPCOBL_CUST` row and passing it to the `CHECK_CUSTOMERFIELDS` parameter of `BAPI_ACCSERV_CHECKACCASSIGNMT`.

a. `READ TABLE BBPCOBL_CUST INDEX SY-TABIX.`

b. `MOVE-CORRESPONDING BBPCOBL_CUST TO CHECK_CUSTOMERFIELDS.`

c. `CALL FUNCTION 'BAPI_ACCSERV_CHECKACCASSIGNMT' EXPORTING ... CHECK_CUSTOMERFIELDS =`

`CHECK_CUSTOMERFIELDS IMPORTING`

To pass the customer fields from the EBP system,

a) Ensure structure BAPICOBL_CI matches the backend structure. If this structure doesn't exist in the EBP system, you may need to create a Z version of it.

b) Add the BBPCOBL_CUST table as an optional parameter to META_ACCSERV_CHECKACCASSIGNMT and any other

*ACCSERVCHECI function modules being used.

c) Where function group BBP_PDACC calls META_ACCSERV_CHECKACCASSIGNMT function, add the relevant code to determine the values to be passed and pass them to the function module. Typically this involves changing both the ACCOUNT CHECK SINGLE (to determine the values) subroutine and the COBL_CHECK (to pass the data) subroutine.

To make ZZEXTRAFLD mandatory, add the mandatory check for ZZEXTRAFLD to the relevant * ACCSERV CHECKACCASSIGNMT function module in EBP

2.0B. In EBP 2.0 you may be able to us a BADI instead.

Ensure the EBP system has OSS note 352511 applied if the global account assignment screen is to be used.

Display ZZEXTRAFLD in Confirmation Account Assignment

To enable the user to see ZZEXTRAFLD in the account assignment display of the confirmation, in Internet service BBPACCOUNT, theme 99, change HTML templates SAPLBBP_PDH_ACC_1 000_CF and SAPLBBPPDHACC_2000_CF to display the ZZEXTRAFLD title and 110 field.

To pick up the ZZEXTRAFLD value from the purchase order, change BAPI_PO_GETDETAIL to return ZZEXTRAFLD, by:

a) Adding ZZEXTRAFLD to structure BAPIEKKN via an append structure.

b) In Include program LMEWPFO4, changing subroutine CEKKN_TO ACCOUNT_ASSIGNMENT. After statement "CLEAR p0_item_account_assignment.", add statement "MOVE-CORRESPONDING cekkn TO p0_item_account_assignment.

In the EBP system, add ZZEXTRAFLD to structure BAPIEKKN via an append structure.

To pass ZZEXTRAFLD from Confirmation to Goods Receipt

No additional changes are required.

To pass ZZEXTRAFLD from Confirmation to Service Entry Sheet

In the backend system, change BAPI_ENTRYSHEETCREATE to accept

ZZEXTRAFLD.

a) Add ZZEXTRAFLD to structure BAPIESKNC and to structure BAPIESKN via append structures.

b) In function module MS_MOVE_BAPIESKN_TQESKN, add line "MOVE CORRESPONDING i_bapieskn to i_eskn." just before the other MOVE statements.

In the EBP system, add ZZEXTRAFLD to structure BAPIESKNC via an append structure.

Transport hints

Transporting Programs, Workflows, Customizing, and other objects is an important part of the SRM system.

The standard transport system should be used for the transport of all client- independent and client-dependent objects.

Change requests can be viewed and released via transaction SEO9.

Transports can be reviewed/continued via transaction STMS. Direct use of operating system commands e.g. "tp" should not be necessary.

Internet services, templates, workflows, and standard tasks are client-independent and are transported in the same way as programs.

Event linkage and start conditions are client-dependent and are transported in the same way as other customizing.

Organizational plans and agent assignment are master data and should not be transported, but instead created in the appropriate system client.

Transporting translations

Transporting translations is via transaction SE63. When entering the translations, "Confirm Translation" creates the transport request. The transport request can then be viewed released via transaction

SE63, menu option "Goto → Administration → Transport recording".

Initially all languages are displayed. Use menu option "Requests → Requests (current language)" to view the transport requests for the current language only. The transport requests must be assigned to a target system prior to release (double-clicking on the transport number will give access to the relevant field). As per normal change requests, transport requests can only be released/changed by the relevant owner.

Transporting ITS services/templates/MIMEs/etc.

Include ITS service/templates/MIMEs/etc. in change requests as normal.

Provided IACOR has been configured and is active for the ITS connected to the target system, transporting the change request to the target system will result in automatic publishing of the ITS related files to the target ITS.

Troubleshooting/debugging hints

Debugging must be turned "ON" for the virtual ITS and a debugging port assigned.

This can be done via the admin service (i.e. remote administration of the ITS).

ITS must be restarted for these settings to take effect.

Create a new SAPLOGON entry with the application server pointing to the ITS Agate machine, and the system number pointing to the debugging port.

Start the relevant web transaction as normal in the web browser. Then double-click on the SAPLOGON entry (from the same PC) and SAPGUI will "piggy-back" on the current ITS session. From this point normal R/3 debugging techniques, e.g. command "/h", can be used.

Note that activity via the web browser will be reflected in SAPGUI but not vice versa. In some situations, using debugging will result in a different behavior to normal on the web browser. For instance, if debugging the call to the catalogue TJRL within SAPGUI, the redirect of the web browser to the catalogue URL determined might not happen as at the time of sending the browser redirect command the connection to the web browser is unclear. Therefore, every effort should be made to get as close to the area of interest in the web transaction prior to starting debugging. E.g. If you want to debug the catalogue URL build, execute the shopping basket creation transaction until just before calling the catalogue prior to connecting to the SAPGUI debug screen.

It is possible to set breakpoints and execute the web transaction to that point. An ITS screen appears indicating that debugging is occurring, and then SAPGUI can be used in the same way to continue the debugging from the break-point. Where soft break points are not possible, modification assistant can be used to insert and remove break point commands.

Debugging Build of Catalog URL

Use ITS debugging to debug from the point of selecting the desired catalogue and pressing the "Go" button. This invokes the ok-code CTLG in program

SAPBBPPU99 that then calls function module BBP_CALL CATALOG.

Hints on Debugging Return of Catalog Data

Return of catalog data invokes the ok-code `ADD!` in program
SAPBBPPU99 that then calls function module BBP The BADI for
manipulating catalog content is called within function module

BBP_GET_CATALOG_CONTENT.

Debugging Vendors

There are several instances that require the verification that vendors are consistent with the backend.

After vendor replication from the backend you will see dummy vendors in the org plan. Should you delete them? There are two philosophies:

1. Live and let live. If it isn't broken, don't fix it. Of course, once it's all working, delete away. I like to take on issues one at a time.

It may happen that your shopping cart is getting stuck at err "Vendor XXXXXX is not intended for purchase org."

2. You may be involved with an upgrade, which from 2.0 to 4.0 gos surprisingly well with one exception ... vendors. The problem is that they are not created in the Org (PPOMA) the correct way for 4.0 to function. If it were up to me, I would send OSS a note to teach you how to delete them from the SRM system. Then re-replicate them from the backend. (I assume we are classic) But to investigate your immediate issue, "Vendor XXXXXX is not intended for purchase org. when the vendors are all yellow" do the following: Login as the

administrator, and go to Edit business partners. Type in the BP number.

(You find the BP number using transaction BP)

If you get the error, BP #___ is not a vendor...then you've got the problem that I alluded to earlier. If not, then go to the vendor tab. (you will undoubtedly need to maintain some pointless data like email address in order to get to the vendor tab). On the vendor tab, you can extend the vendor to the PORG.

CRM_OM_BP_INTEGRATE can be used to check on the vendors. You use BBPGETVD to replicate them BBPGETVC to bring over more data like terms of payment. BBPUPDVD to update vendor records.

Also se37, BBP_VENDOR_GETDETAIL can help you research these guys...

If you have on-going trouble finding out the cause of the vendors not being vendors in SRM, then you can compare two systems.

Debugging Workflow

Advice on debugging workflow can be found in OSS notes 329564 and 322526.

In particular the following program should be added to the EBP system:

REPORT Z_BASKET_LINKS.

DATA: BEGIN OF objkey, objtype(10) type c value 'BUS2121',

objval(70) type c,

END OF objkey. PARAMETERS: basket LIKE reqhead-reqno. objkey-objval = basket.

SUBMIT rswioins AND RETURN with object eq objkey.

This program allows entry of a shopping basket number and returns the workflows and work items related to this shopping basket. Double-clicking on workflow lines opens the workflow log for deeper debugging.

The shopping basket number can be found in the "Change and Check Status" web transaction, in the basic data of the shopping basket item.

If Z_BASKET_LINKS finds NO work items for a shopping basket:

a) Check that the shopping basket was ordered and not parked (held).

b) Check the start conditions for the workflows — every shopping basket must find one and only one shopping basket workflow that has an active event linkage.

If Z_BASKET_LINKS finds multiple workflows for a shopping basket:

a) Check the start conditions for the workflows — every shopping basket must find one and only one shopping basket workflow that has an active event linkage.

b) Check that the shopping basket number range has not been reset.

If Z_BASKET_LINKS find one and only workflow, and the workflow log shows that the workflow has completed successfully, then THE PR OBLEM IS NOT IN WORKFLOW!!!

Note that the final step in the approval workflow is to start the shopping basket transfer routine (function module BBP_REQREQTRANSFER). Proble ms in this routine can affect the approval status display on the web even if the workflow was executed successfully. In particular, if the shopping basket is still in "awaiting approval" status even though it has been approved via the workflow, this indicates that the BBP_REQREQTRANSFER routine was unable to complete processing of the shopping basket.

If BBP_REQREQ_TRANSFER has failed, messages should appear on the application monitors. It is also possible to debug the failure using transaction SE37 to run BBP_REQREQTRANSFER in test mode against the affected shopping basket.

Debugging Backend Object Choice

Create a shopping basket but HOLD (park) it, but don't order it.

Use SE37 to test function module BBP_REQREQ_TRANSFER.
Execute (with no RFCDESTINATION) and debug from that point.
The RFCDESTINATION is assumes as the source client.

Debugging Initial Creation of Follow on Documents

Create a shopping cart but place it on HOLD, do not order it.

Use the function module builder, transaction se37, to execute function BBP_REQREQTRANSFER and debug from this point on.

Debugging Failure to Create a Backend Object

Use transaction SE16 with table REQREF to find the backend object type and backend object number reference for the shopping basket/item(s) involved.

Backend object types:

BUS2105 = Purchase requisition

BUS2012 = Purchase order

BUS2093 = Reservation

Function modules:

For earlier EBP versions

SPOOL_REQ_CREATE_DO for purchase requisitions

SPOOL_PU_CREATE_DO for purchase orders

SPOOL_RS CREATE DO for reservations

<u>For EBP 4.0</u>

BBP_PO_SC_TRANSFER

BBP_PD_SC_RESUBMIT

Depending on the backend object type, using transaction SE37 "Test" mode input the shopping basket number and backend object reference number to the matching function module and debug from that point.

For Confirmations (Goods Receipts):

Goods Receipts are passed via ALE.

Backend object type is BUS2017.

Use transaction WE05 in the EBP and backend systems to see what has happened to the IDOC. The "Status" section of the IDOC display gives any error/success messages.

For Confirmations (Service Entry Sheets):

Get the GUID reference from table BBP_PDBEH.

Backend object type is BUS2O91.

Function module is SPOOL_ES_CREATE_DO.

Debugging transactions/programs from SAPG UI

By granting debug authority (via authority object S_DEVELOP) to a test EBP user, such as an employee, it is often possible to logon to SAPGUI as that user and execute the relevant transaction in SAPGUI only, ABAP debugging as normal.

For instance, most of the confirmations transaction BBPCFO2 can be executed directly via SAPGUI.

As EBP transactions are usually marked as "Easy Web Transactions" and therefore cannot be started via the standard SAP Easy Access menu, it is necessary to use command "/N" to move

away from the SAP Easy Access menu before calling the
transaction from the command line.

Troubleshooting Application Monitor messages

Shopping Basket Error: "Partner master data" or "invalid address"

Run transaction CRM_OM_BP_INTEGRATE for the shopping basket creator's org unit. Check that an org unit address has been correctly created.

Run transaction CRMM_BP for the shopping basket creator's contact person (i.e. Business Partner id assigned to the shopping basket creator). On the "Relationships" tab, drill down on the BTJRO1O ("is employee of") relationship to the org unit's business partner id. The org unit address should be displayed. If not, repeat these steps with CRPVIIM BP in "change" mode, and when drilled down on the org unit business partner, "Assign comp.address" to link the org unit address to the employee to org unit relationship.

Checking on Invoices

WE05 – IDOC processing

BD87 – If an Idoc is stuck, you can fix the error and re-process sometimes

FB03 is display of purchasing docs.

Go to Display, and find the internal Invoice number from the CoCode, Fiscal Year, and Reference Key (the SRM doc number)

Distribution Model for ALE

BD64, create model, then create message types for:

ACC_GOODS_MOVEMENT

ACLPAY

ACPJMM

BBPCO

BBPIV

MBGMCR

Then Generate partner profiles

Then Model view -> distribute

NOTE: When you copy these from another system, you will need to delete the old model and delete the existing entries in table EDP13. This table contains PORTS and links to RFC destinations, which are system and client specific.

You will need to let the system regenerate the PORTS to the correct RFC destination.

JIM STEWART

Removing PIRS from Sourcing Consideration

It is possible to disregard inforecords for sourcing purposes in R/3. If you do so EBP will automatically disregard inforecords as well. This approach consistently removes info-records as sources of supply in both, R/3 and EBP. Here's how:

1. Run cmod transaction in R/3 and create your project

2. Assign enhancement LMEQR001 to your project

3. In component EXIT_SAPLMEQR_001 there is include

ZXM06U52 and you need to enter some code in this include. Here is an example how to remove ALL inforecords:

```
*--------------------------*
*  INCLUDE ZXM06U52 *
*--------------------------*
loop at t_sources.
if not t_sources-infnr is initial.
```

```
delete t_sources index sy-tabix.
endif.
endloop.
```

Note: BBP_SOS_BADI can only be used for customizing the searches of local sources of supply: local contracts, vendor lists and or vendor linkages.

Forcing Preferred Vendor to Fixed Vendor

Implement the following method, in which you will force vendor to "fixed vendor" for all applicable shopping carts.

IF_EX_BBP_DOC_CHANGE_BADI~BBP_SC_CHANGE.

You will have to work with partner function '00000039' which is the preferred vendor to move it into partner function '00000019' which is the fixed vendor

In the BBP_DOC_CHANGE_BADI we provide the business partner data through the
IT_PARTNER interface table. The preferred vendor or desired vendor has
partner type 39. The regular supplier will have partner type 19. A switch
from 39 to 19 should create a PO instead of requisition

Changing email templates

If you want to change the template of the emails that are sent out when you create a new user for a Business Partner

Transaction SE61.

Document text = General text

Document name = PARTNER REQUEST ACCEPTED

Service providers

A service provider is a user created for a business partner.

When you go into business partner administration to create a contact person for a business partner you choose to create

a. Contact Person OR

b. Service Provider OR

c. Both (by checking both check-boxes)

Finding EBP Messages

Table T100

Message class BBP_PD, BBP_WFL, etc.

Examples:

BBP_WFL 013, Approval workflow is ambiguous. Inform system administrator
BBP_PD 488, Current document status does not permit this action

Tax Jurisdiction code messages

 Reference to Note: 650893   Message class TAX_TXJCD
Customizable message

All that was required was to edit V_T100C and turn off message 105 for

TAX_TXJCD.

 FM for vendor review: BBP_BUPA_XPRA_30A

Creating the Org Plan

Check the Business Partner (BP) – the address data was not included in the business partner creation. This can happen when you save an Org before adding the address.

You may need to run se38: CRM_MKTBP_ZCACL_UPDATE_30

Those orgs with the error may still need to have the address manually added in the BP but all new Orgs should behave correctly.

Changing the logical system of a backend for client copy

The issue here is that the master data (plants, product categories / material groups, BASIS3) from a different backend than the one to be used.

1. First basis should perform the copy and run BDLS.

2. Fix the configuration, such as "Define backend systems" etc.

3. Plants: They can be deleted from BBP_LOCMAP (Se16).

4. Re-run DNL_CUST_* downloads.

You may get an error: LOGSYS_FOR_GUID_CHANGED in the inbound queue in EBP (smq2).

In this case, the system is complaining because it set the GUID of the backend system to a different logical system.

Go to table CRMMLSGUID and delete the entry from the table.

5. Finally, to fix the attributes, run se38: RHOMATTRIBUTES_REPLACE.

This will present all of the attributes with corresponding Org units. You can enter the OLD and NEW logical system names.

Workflow advanced tips

Run transaction SWLD - go to the WF Builder.

Enter in the WF that is activated, and you can drill into it.

Anchors=sub Workflows

Arrows=Tasks

Background processing does not allow agent assignment – it is a system step – do not mess with these.

After changes are made, insure that you "Refresh Index" and perform a "Syntax check" for each screen. Then at the last screen, you can "Activate" the WF with the changes.

P Cards (Purchasing Cards)

In the standard delivery, it is not possible to enter procurement card as a payment method when using Enterprise Buyer is implemented in a "classic" scenario. Since the shopping cart does not contain procurement card information, it is not possible to pass this information on to the backend documents such as purchase requisitions and purchase orders in a "classic" scenario.

Update Status of Shopping Carts

You may find that even though you've initiated a transfer of a shopping cart to the back end, when you check the status of the shopping cart with bbp_pd, or via the web, that nothing has changed. This is probably because the update status jobs haven't run.

To manually/immediately update information in EBP documents, run:

Se37: BBP_REQREQ_TRANSFER (transfers doc to backend)

SE38: BBP_GET_STATUS_2 (Updates info into EBP)

Se37: RHOMATTRIBUTES_CONSISTENCY

Look for HRT5500 / 5505 table and repair this.

It is caused by large changes in the Org Structure and messes up the Db call for these org elements (like Purchasing groups and Purchasing Orgs)

Fixing the Org Structure and Users

Organizational synchronization – Fix Orgs

Transaction: CRM_OM_BP_INTEGRATE

Users assign to Org, fixes users

Transaction: USERS_GEN

Maintain Attribute inheritance

Se37: T770MATTR

EBP Administrator via SAPGUI

Transaction: RZ20

Approve Shopping Cart via SAPGUI

Run transaction SE37:
BBP_PDH_WFL_APPROVAL_SIMULATE

Enter BUS2121 and SC#

Copy Work Item Number (i.e. 25230)

SWI1: Enter WI# into Identification

Ensure Personal Settings have flagged

Enable forwarding to others

Use all objects

Technical views

Edit->Change

Complete manually (Status changed to "completed")

Also note SWI5 to view work item

You must have personal workflow settings indicate "technical view" – otherwise you cannot change the work item.

To find Web Template name

From webpage, right-click and view source

To Shop via SAPGUI

Login as user, transaction: BBPSC01

Data Replication

Troubleshooting tips for Data Replication in EBP40 (with 4.5B backend) applies to EBP 5.0 as well.

1.   CRMRFCPAR table contains entry for <yourRFCDEST> for CRM user. (Only one entry should exist)

2.   CRM site - added link to EBP's logical system name <yourRFCDEST>

2.   Start download r3as

3.   Monitor download r3am1

4.   Release queue in R3 – smq1

5.   Release queue in EBP – smq2 **
6.   So…to repeat, we cancelled download in r3am1

7.   Delete queue R3A_DNL_CUST_BASIS3 in EBP smq2 but kept R3A* and the other wildcard Qs. This can also cause a problem 8. Restart download

9.   Delete all queues in smq2 (including all wildcard Qs)

10.   Restart download, release queue in R3 and EBP…all worked.

Also check:

tables CRMCONSUM, TBE11, CRMPAROLTP in R3 backend

Set up Sites: CRM using BBP_PRODUCT_SETTINGS_MW and manually setup backend site type R/3 with properties connected to R/3 destination

Sites must be linked to logical system name (SMOEAC)

User must have SAPCRM_MENUE authorization

Batch job for delta MATERIAL replication, use ABAP program SMOF_DOWNLOAD

SMWP and SMW01 can give detailed error reports

Note: Once time we had the system ID incorrectly configured for the RFC destination and it created the queue in the sending system (the R3 system) instead of in the EBP system.

HTML Changes

Run transaction in GUI, i.e. BBPSC01

If you can't run the transaction directly, make sure to type /n to exit any transaction. You can also try running the transaction via se93.

When you run BBPSC01, you can select technical details, and get technical info, template and screen name.

Another trick is to use the shopping cart from the web, find the field on the web page, and "View Source" by right clicking in the appropriate area. Take care that due to many subscreens, you must click in just the right place to get the source code you may be going after.

Edit template: Internet Services (se80) for EBP – that contain the templates that we changed:

BBPSC01

BBPGLOBAL

BBPSEARCH

BBPACCOUNT

*Must save and republish after making changes

Appendix A: Transaction Codes

BBP0	Start Menu for SAP B2B Procurement
BBPADDREXT	Maintain Vendor Address - External
BBPADDRINTC	Maintain Addresses for Own Company
BBPADDRINTV	Maintain Vendor Address (Internal)
BBPADM_COCKPIT	Administrator Monitor Dummy
BBPADM_MONITOR	Flow Logic Service BBPADM_MONITOF
BBPAPPL	Define EBP Applications
BBPAPPL_DISP	Define EBP Applications
BBPAPPL_TRSP	Define EBP Applications
BBPAT02	Parameter ID tree maintenance
BBPAT03	Create User
BBPAT04	Forgotten User ID/Password
BBPAT05	Change User Data
BBPATTRMAINT	Maintain Attributes
BBPAVLMAINT	AVL Maintenance (Display / Change)
BBPBC1	XML invoice transfer
BBPBWSC1	SC Analyses for Manager (Old)
BBPBWSP	Start Enterprise Buyer Inbox
BBPBWSP_SIMPLE	Start Enterprise Buyer Inbox
BBPCACC	Maintain Account Assign. Categories
BBPCF01	GR/SE for Vendor

BBPCF02	GR/SE for Desktop User
BBPCF03	Goods Recpt/Serv.for Profession.User
BBPCF04	Confirmation Approval
BBPCF05	Carry Out Review for Confirmation
BBPCMSG1	Customizing Flexible Message Control
BBPCMSG2	XML Message Control
BBPCTOL	Maintain Tolerances
BBPCU04	Set Up Default Workflows
BBPCU05	Link Manager to Org. Structure
BBPCU06	Link Administrator to Org. Structure
BBPCU07	Current Role for User Generation
BBPCU08	Workflow Wizard
BBPDIFF	Version Comparison
BBPGETVD	Transfer Vendor Master
BBPGLOBAL	Transaction for Internet Transaction
BBPHELP	Help for Specific Transactions
BBPINSTALLCOUNTRIES	Activate country-specific EBP field
BBPINSTALLSZENARIO	Installation of CUF Scenarios
BBPIV01	Vendor User Invoice Input
BBPIV02	Desktop User Invoice Input
BBPIV03	Prof. User Invoice Input
BBPIV04	Invoice Approval
BBPIV05	Perform Invoice Review
BBPIV06	Change Incorrect XML Invoice
BBPMAINAPP	Startup for Vendor Approval

BBPMAINEXT	Process Vendor or Bidder
BBPMAININT	Process Vendor or Bidder
BBPMAINMANAGER	Process own Company (only)
BBPMAINNEW	Request Vendor or Bidder
BBPMAINPURCH	Process own Purch.Org. View (only)
BBPMONSTART	Start the BBP monitors
BBPOR01	Component Planning for Orders
BBPOR02	Post processing Orders
BBPPCO01	PCO: Prof. User
BBPPCO02	Purchase Order Response: Entered By
BBPPCO_PO	Purchase Order Confirmation: Call P
BBPPCO_WF	Purchase Order Confirmation: Call W
BBPPO01	Purchaser Cockpit
BBPPS01	Component Planning for Projects
BBPPS02	Post processing Projects
BBPPU07	Manager Inbox
BBPPU08	Employee Inbox
BBPPU09	Administrator Cockpit
BBPPU12	Reviewer Inbox
BBPRP01	Reporting, Data Retrieval from Core
BBPSC01	Shopping Cart - Full Functionality
BBPSC02	Shopping Cart - Wizard
BBPSC03	Shopping Cart - Limited Functions
BBPSC04	Shopping Cart Status
BBPSC05	Public Template (Create)
BBPSC06	Public Template (Change)
BBPSC07	Manager Inbox
BBPSC08	Employee Inbox
BBPSC09	Administrator Cockpit
BBPSC10	Reviewer Inbox
BBPSC11	Shopping Cart Display Item Overview
BBPSC12	Shopping Cart Display Item Details
BBPSC13	Change Shopping Cart
BBPSC14	SC Display for Rec. Management

BBPSC15	SC Display for CFolder
BBPSC16	SC Number of Itm Det. for CFolder
BBPSC17	SC Number of Itm Det. for Rec. Mgmt
BBPSC18	Request Temporary Staff
BBPSC19	Request External Staff (Change)
BBPSHOWVD	Display vendor data
BBPSOCO01	Sourcing Cockpit
BBPSR01	Service Entry (Component)
BBPSR02	Entry Sheet Maintenance (Component)
BBPST01	Start EBR Menu
BBPST02	Start EBR Menu
BBPSTART1	Flow Logic Service BBPSTART
BBPSUBSCRIBE	Add additional subscriber user data
BBPTRACE	Switch on EBP Trace
BBPTRACK	Status Tracking: Call Structure
BBPUPDVD	Update Vendor Master Record
BBPUSERMAINT	user Maintain
BBPU_IAC_TEST	Test Transaction for ITS
BBPVE01	Vendor Evaluation
BBPVENDOR	BBP Vendor Logon
BBPWEBMONITOR	Application Monitor w/o Flow Logic
BBPWEBMON_SEP	Monitor in New Window
BBPWI	Central Initial Screen WI Execution
BBPWLRA01	Workload Reassignment
BBP_ARCH_RESI	Define EBP Residence Times
BBP_ATTR_CHECK	EBP Organizational Model: Checks
BBP_AUCTION	BBP Live Auction
BBP_AUC_SRM_EX	Live Auction Return from Applet
BBP_BE_LIST	Vendor List
BBP_BGRD_APPROVAL	Background Approval
BBP_BID_EVAL	EBP Bid Evaluation
BBP_BID_EXTSO	Display Bid Invitation from SOCO
BBP_BID_INV	BBP Bid Invitation Cockpit

BBP_BP_OM_INTEGRA TE	Integration BP Orgmanagement
BBP_BW_SC2	SB Monitoring Admin (PD)
BBP_BW_SC3	Shopping Carts per Product
BBP_BW_SC4	Shopping Carts per Cost Center
BBP_CCM_TRANSFER	Data Transfer to Catalog
BBP_CFOLDER	Redirect from cFolders
BBP_CHECK_USERS	Check EBP Users
BBP_CLEANER	Start Synchronization with Backend
BBP_CND_CHECK	Check Conditions Customizing
BBP_CND_CHECK_CU ST	Check Conditions Customizing
BBP_CONT_ACTION_D EF	Define Action Profiles
BBP_CTR_DISP	Contract in Display Mode
BBP_CTR_DISPNR	Display Contract without Return
BBP_CTR_EXT_PO	Display Contract from PO and SOC
BBP_CTR_EXT_WF	Display Contract from Workflow
BBP_CTR_MAIN	Process Contracts
BBP_CTR_MAINCC	Process Global Outline Agreement
BBP_CTR_MON	Monitor Contract Distribution
BBP_CTR_SEARCC	Find Global Outline Agreement
BBP_CTR_WF_APP	Branch from Approval Workflow
BBP_CTR_WF_CHG	Branch Contract from Change Workflow
BBP_CT_SCM_STAGIN G	Staging UI for Schema Import
BBP_CT_STAGING	Staging
BBP_CUST_CAT	Call Structure Maint. of Catalogs
BBP_CUST_DET_ACCT	Determine G/L Account by Category
BBP_CUST_DET_LOGS YS	Determine Target System by Category
BBP_CUST_LOGSYS	Maintenance of the Backend System
BBP_CUST_TARGET_O BJ	MMaint. of Objects to Be Generated
BBP_CUS_ACCESS_SE	EBP: Define Access Sequences

Q

BBP_DYN_ATTR_EDIT	Maintenance of Dynamic Attributes
BBP_EVAL_SURVEY	Survey Cockpit
BBP_GETCD_ITS	Display Change Documents
BBP_MON	Open the Monitor Display
BBP_MON_SC	Monitor Shopping Cart
BBP_MS_ACC_DET_C	Multiple Company: Acct for Category
BBP_MS_BE_C	Multiple Company: Maintain FI Backend
BBP_MS_MAP_TAX_C	Multiple Company: Tax Code
BBP_MS_MSG1_C	Message Control
BBP_MS_MSG2_C	Multiple Company: Flex. Message XML
BBP_MS_STD_ACC_C	MultipleCompany:LocalAcctAssigmtDat
BBP_NUM_AUC	Number Range Maintenance 'AUC'
BBP_NUM_AVL	Number Range Definition 'AVL'
BBP_NUM_BID	Bid Invitation Nr Range Maintenance
BBP_NUM_CONF	Procure. Confirm. Nr Range Mainten.
BBP_NUM_INV	Invoice Number Range Maintenance
BBP_NUM_INVD	Number Ranges for Invoice Template
BBP_NUM_PC	No.Range Maint. Contrct/Del.Schedul
BBP_NUM_PCO	Number Range Maint for NkObj POCONF
BBP_NUM_PO	Purchase Order Nr Range Maintenance
BBP_NUM_QUOT	Bid Number Range Maintenance
BBP_NUM_SUSASN	Number Range Maintenance: 'SUSASN'
BBP_NUM_SUSCF	Number Ranges Maintenance: 'SUSPO'
BBP_NUM_SUSINV	Number Ranges for 'SUSINV'
BBP_NUM_SUSPCO	Number Ranges for 'SUSPCO'
BBP_NUM_SUSPO	Number Ranges Maintenance: 'SUSPO'
BBP_OCI_AGENT	Cross-Catalog Search
BBP_OM_TRANSL	Translate Organizational Units
BBP_PCCOM	PCard Commitment Customizing
BBP_PD	Document Display (EBP)
BBP_PDH_TEXT	bbp_pdh_text
BBP_PD_PO_ERRORL OG	Starts Entry Screen for Error Log

BBP_PM01	Postman scenario
BBP_POC	Process Purchase Orders
BBP_POC_DISPLY	Display Transaction for the PO
BBP_POC_WF_APP	Approval Transaction for the PO
BBP_POC_WF_REQ	Approval PO for Requester
BBP_POC_WF_REV	Approval PO for Reviewer
BBP_PO_ACTION_CON F	Configure Action Conditions
BBP_PO_ACTION_DEF	Define Action Profiles
BBP_PPF	Output Control Purchase Order
BBP_PPF_CONT	Trigger Selection Contracts
BBP_PPF_OLD	PO Trigger Administration
BBP_PRODUCT_SETTI NG	BBP with/without CRM
BBP_QUOT	Create Bid
BBP_QUOT_EXTST	Display Bid from Status
BBP_QUOT_EXTWF	Display Bid Invitation -> Bid fr. WF
BBP_SC_DARKAPP_IA C	Approve Shopping Cart in Background
BBP_SNEW_SYNCVD	Shows New Vendor Repl. from Backend
BBP_SP_COMP_INI	Replication of Companies & Employees
BBP_SP_SUPP_INI	Download Vendors for Service Portal
BBP_SUPP_MONI	Vendor Monitor
BBP_SUS_BP_ADM	Management of Business Partners
BBP_TRIGG	Output Actions
BBP_TRIGG_CTR	Output Contract
BBP_TRIGG_ERS	Output ERS Document
BBP_TRIGG_INV	Output Invoice
BBP_TRIGG_MEN	Output Document

JIM STEWART

ABOUT THE AHTHOR

Jim Stewart (Los Angeles, CA) has over 10 years of
experience as an SAP consultant, during which time he has
served as a functional lead, lead developer, and ABAP
programmer. He has implemented SAP for The US Army,
DirecTV, Texas Instruments, Hewlett Packard, and other
Fortune 100 clients. Mr. Stewart is the founder of Equity
Technology Group, an SAP consulting partner, and continues
to practice as a consultant in the area of SAP SRM,
Workflow, Web programming, and UNIX systems
administration. Equity Technology Group is a leading
provider of SRM implementation support and services.

Equity Technology Group

Tel: 951-788-0810

Fax: 951-788-0812

Email: fjstewart@equitytechgroup.com

www.equitytechgroup.com

<u>NOTES</u>

<u>NOTES</u>

<u>NOTES</u>

NOTES

<u>NOTES</u>

<u>NOTES</u>

<u>NOTES</u>

<u>NOTES</u>

<u>NOTES</u>

<u>NOTES</u>

www.ingramcontent.com/pod-product-compliance
Lightning Source LLC
Chambersburg PA
CBHW051224050326
40689CB00007B/797